Enough Light for the Next Step:

A Memoir of Love, Loss, and Spirit

Annie Wenger-Nabigon, Ph.D.

Library and Archives Canada Cataloguing in Publication

Title: Enough light for the next step : a memoir of love, loss, and spirit / by Annie
    Wenger-Nabigon.
Names: Wenger-Nabigon, Annie E., author.
Identifiers: Canadiana 20220131724 | ISBN 9781988989440 (softcover)
Subjects: LCSH: Wenger-Nabigon, Annie E. | LCSH: Nabigon, Herb. | LCSH: Wenger-Nab-
igon, Annie E.—
    Marriage. | LCSH: Social workers—Ontario, Northern—Biography. | LCSH: College
teachers—Ontario,
    Northern—Biography. | LCSH: Ontario, Northern—Biography. | CSH: Authors, Canadian
(English)—
    Ontario, Northern—Biography. | CSH: First Nations—Ontario, Northern—Biography. |
LCGFT:
    Autobiographies.
Classification: LCC HV40.32.W46 A3 2022 | DDC 361.3092—dc23

Printed and bound in Canada on 100% recycled paper.
Cover Design: Chippy Joseph
Author photo: Tammy Fiegehen

Published by:
Latitude 46 Publishing
info@latitude46publishing.com
Latitude46publishing.com

The production of this book was made possible through the generous assistance of the Ontario Arts Council. We would also like to acknowledge the support of the Government of Canada through the Canada Book Fund and the Ontario Government through the Ontario Book Fund.

ONTARIO ARTS COUNCIL
CONSEIL DES ARTS DE L'ONTARIO
an Ontario government agency
un organisme du gouvernement de l'Ontario

Funded by the
Government
of Canada | Canadä

Enough Light for the Next Step:

A Memoir of Love, Loss, and Spirit

Annie Wenger-Nabigon, Ph.D.

46

For Herb

and for our children,
Rachel, Kathy (Annie)
Clem and Alana (Herb)

Contents

INTRODUCTION

OUR MISSING LIVES

The story I want to tell you is of my life with Herb Nabigon, an Elder and member of the Loon Clan of the Anishnaabeg peoples. His name was Maahng-ese, Little Loon. He walked this Earth for almost 74 years, the last ten of them with me at his side. This is a story of the love and spirit that walked with us in our lives—the poetry and metaphor of living beyond the bounds of human loss.

Many parts of the story elude me. Their shape keeps changing, the light around me keeps changing, the world tilts and shifts until I need to stand still and close my eyes to stop the dizzying whirl of confused thoughts and memories. Can my inner vision grow calm if I'm just still enough? When I open my eyes again, will I still feel just as blind, as if I'm groping in the darkness for a handhold, seeking something familiar to help me place myself, relieved to finally find my life again? Will there be, please, enough light for the next step?

I breathe in. Breathe out. It is never the same breath, never the same moment. How can I reconstruct that which is gone? How can I tell you about that which takes the shape of feelings without words? How can I reconstruct the story of our missing life together? What is my intention for my life now that he has travelled on? So much is missing from my life now that he is gone. I grieve the loss of our life together.

If I could tell you what I wished to share, I would start with the pictures in my mind, and I would begin with this: my office where I worked when we met and the beautiful tree outside the window that I loved; the little grey cat who lived at my house, peeking out from behind the couch the first time Herb came to visit; the Sweat Lodge in an Indiana countryside where I realized there was going to be more to this connection; the many hours at John and Beth's simple farmhouse where our joy overflowed in happy conversations; the trip to meet his family in Canada at Christmas when he told me we would only have ten years together—the Elders had told him when his lifespan on this Earth would come to an end; the wedding event at Burwash Landing, Ontario, out in the bush under a sacred arbor with the Pipe Carriers and family and friends gathered beneath the trees; the road trip through Ontario and Pennsylvania for a month after our wedding, checking in to several family reunions; the questions I asked which he could not answer; the stories he shared of his childhood in the bush, the life of a trapper's son; the dark times of Residential and Day School that formed the early years of his formal education; the train accident that took his arm; the poignant markers in a life with years of lost memory; the narratives he constructed to fill in the blanks when he couldn't piece together what was lost— narratives he needed to create for a logical connection to what was real.

It turned out that we were both the real connection for each other, holding fast to a life that expanded together, even as the physical trajectory curved to an ending. It is expanding still...

If I could make it possible for you to hear his voice speaking in calm, melodic tones and his captivating, full-bodied laugh, I would start with his own words on the topic closest to his heart:

> *"Indigenous knowledge can help us learn how to heal humanity and the Earth. The tens of thousands of years of accumulated wisdom from the Elders and the Ancestors call us to reactivate the circle of relationships in the natural world and among people. This will take time and effort by each soul . . . Indigenous knowledge can help guide us to a place of healing, learning, growing and relating in a better way to Mother Earth and among us all."*

Herb had a passion for sharing Indigenous knowledge, the traditional teachings of his people, which had healed him from losing his life to alcohol. He believed strongly that the teachings, rooted in a connection to Mother Earth, were for everyone, all the directions and colours of the races of humankind represented on the Medicine Wheel. When Herb talked of Mother Earth, he often used the Ojibway word, *Shkagamik-Kwe.* In his wisdom, he knew that we were all Her children.

He loved Mother Earth and longed for people to take better care of Her, of the beautiful Garden of this planet. He identified the colour green as representative of Her and believed in Her healing powers. He loved the colour green and could talk for hours about traditional teachings connected with this colour. His final words in this life were "Green, like Mother Earth," spoken to his daughter not long before his last breath.

Listening to his teachings over and over during the ten years we were together shaped my inner territory into a vast space that is at the same time both easy *and* difficult to live with. Missing him is a journey that I will always travel, but the gifts he left help reveal a path ahead.

I'm still an infant on this journey...

I'm on a meandering path to understand this story, this life without his physical presence. It's as if I am creating it with bits of cloth to stitch together, trying to create a warm, comforting quilt of memories. Sometimes the story folds back upon itself, as quilts are folded, layered for warmth, or stored for safekeeping. My feelings about it all are shaded by my desire to hold fast to the powerful love we shared. I nurture my intention to live the life ahead of me in a strong way, carrying the traditional teachings he shared with me, and sharing that wisdom with others.

One day, when we were standing in the kitchen of our new home at Pic River First Nation, he turned and smiled at me with tears in his eyes and said, "Annie, I don't know what I'd do without you. I'd be lost without you. I think all I could do would be to get a few bottles of rye and buy a room at the Delta Chelsea and drink myself to death."

I was shocked at this statement and reacted, "Herbert Nabigon! Why on Earth would you say such a thing? Don't you dare do that—if you do, I'll come back to haunt you!"

Then we had a conversation about loss and pain, need and love ... it was always about love. There were not enough ways to express that love, and the old fear of abandonment that lurked in the background, the one I understood so very well, left an opening for the haunt of alcoholism to raise its ugly head. The stories of our lives needed careful telling to keep the shape of healing.

After 36 years of sobriety, alcohol was still the thought that came to him when considering the possibility of the intolerable pain of separation, and the instinct to run from that pain was so great that escape was all he could imagine in the moment's intensity. We needed our relationship to remind us of the Teachings that gave our life structure and grounded us in the face of impending loss, which all humans must face, again, and again, and ever again.

When he died, the last thing he said to me was, "Annie, I love you so much." That tender phrase teaches me over and over what I have to treasure, what I have to pass on. I find tears close to the surface as I remember his voice speaking those precious last words to me. I recognize it as a treasure that not everyone experiences in their life, and I honour that with respect and humility.

I'm glad I'm the one left to carry that pain of loss. He had already carried more than a whole nation could handle. He hadn't signed up for any of that, but it came anyway. Now he is gone from this walk, and I travel on, trying to find a way to remember all I can, and share what I have learned. I have words and pictures. I can piece this together like a crazy quilt, and the quilt could grow and grow, until it's large enough to cover the Washington Mall where he told me he once heard a man named Martin talk of a dream. I don't know what parts of that story are woven with fact, but I know there's a truth to our dream together that I want to share. The dream is a quilt of love spreading out through time, forward and backward, folding in on itself through an endless loving universe.

We lived a dream. It was *our* dream. When he left to travel, as he believed, to the Creator's home, I was the age he had been when he met me, and I have years to live before I reach the age he was at death. The years that pass bring me closer to the journey he's on, the mystery he entered into, but it's the same eternal now in which we all live.

Annie Wenger-Nabigon
May 2019

PROLOGUE

The first year after Herb's death, I felt as if I were living with a heart amputation. In an odd way, I felt even closer to him because I believed I could now identify better with the arm amputation he had lived with for over 50 years.

I believe now that by dwelling on the metaphor of an "amputated heart" to express my grief, I contributed to the heart health challenges I had in the following years. Changing that thought has helped me to redirect self-caring energies into creating a new home within my heart.

In reality, nothing was amputated in my life. It's just a way of expressing the wrenching loss I experience now that he isn't with us any longer. It seems as if life without his physical presence is like the phantom limb pain that he lived with for so long. I've learned, though, that loss can be as much an illusion as anything else in life. Embracing it brings unexpected transformation, and a wisdom that opens the heart to gratitude and joy.

Sometimes, now, I wonder: do the losses of our lives become heart amputations that fester and cause the hardness and mistakes in our lives? Is that the beginning of the spark of life disappearing and taking with it all connections to our true selves? Is that why so many people seem lost in this life? Herb healed from his amputations—both that of his arm and those in his heart—and he shared his healing knowledge generously. My brain was healed after the serious accident I had in 2003 (two years before I met him) and my life healed through the gifts that Spirit brought to me through that experience. Creator's power was manifested through the healing in our lives. It's the story of this precious gift that I want to share.

A few weeks before I moved out of the home where we had shared the last four years of his life, I woke from a dream, startled, surprised, and quite frustrated with Herb. He had come to me in the dream, walking towards me, smiling and waving, and I felt so happy to see him again. He had both of his arms and was joyful and excited. I thought he would stop and talk with me and hug me, but he called out, "Hi, Annie!" and kept walking very fast past me. He turned around as he walked away and continued to wave as I pivoted to watch him. He called out, "I'm going to find some cedar for you!" Maybe I'll need a lot of cedar to get into Creator's home! He was so happy, with that wonderful, carefree smile on his face that I loved so much. Herb really knew how to be happy.

Waking from the dream was intense. Ambivalence overwhelmed me. I truly felt as if he had been right there with me, but I was upset that he hadn't stopped to talk with me and hold me. Then I laughed. Of course! He was, as ever, occupied with what was important to him, and cedar was one of the most important medicines he used. *Gizhgaatig*, the Tree of Light, lit the way to the Sweat Lodge, showing the trail to the Creator's home. It was a sacred Medicine that was used for protection, for healing, for cleansing. It was the traditional medicine that we burned on the sacred fire in the four days following his death, in keeping with his wishes for the old ceremonies of the Anishnaabeg to be conducted following his death. Herb always seemed to know what was most important. Keep it simple.

And wouldn't you know, magnificent cedar trees grow everywhere around the new place I live. Wherever I go, I see cedar trees. Herb has a unique way of making himself known. He sends me pennies too, and nickels, dimes, quarters, Loonies, and Toonies, finding coins in unexpected places, sometimes daily, or weekly, or monthly. That rarely happened to me before he died.

At this time in my life, many things are changing. It's a marvellous and challenging journey to walk the spiral from birth to death through this physical world. Sometimes, it seems to be a journey designed to terrify me, but it always inspires me. I'm so grateful for the life I shared with this special partner whose memory comforts me. The gratitude heals me.

I feel Herb walking with me in the Spirit World, and while I know he has moved on to do whatever it is that spirits do, I'm also conscious that he is with me, as are all our ancestors, all the spirits, and especially *Gzhemnidoo*, the Creator, the Great Spirit—*G'Chi-Manitou*. I am at peace while also continuing to deeply experience the grief arising from the wrenching pain of no longer having Herb by my side. His spirit and mine work together to help me, but tears still sometimes burst with waves of raw despair, and, for a while, some days felt very hard to navigate. Good work helps, and friends and family who understand and support me carry me through. This is the path carrying me forward in these years.

I'm the caterpillar melting in the cocoon, slowly morphing into a larger life, waiting for my wings to grow, unfold, and dry, ready to soar.

I hope sharing the story of our life together and the teachings he passed onto me will help make him known to you. I hope our story will offer just enough light for the next step to the home within your heart.

In the Beginning

Not many people who know me truly understand the backstory of my life with Herb and what it is that seamlessly ties me into the final stage of his life. A few people know bits and pieces, fragments of my story, but a rarer few have comprehended how far a journey I travelled to be in a life with Herb. It seems incongruous, unlikely—how could someone from my background come to fit so intimately into a life with this Anishnaabe Elder? It is an intricate puzzle.

Family and relatives, and some friends, know parts of my origin story—the birthplace in the mountains of north central Arkansas in the traditional territory of the Osage nation. I lived in an isolated Mennonite medical mission site consisting of a school, a church, and a clinic building where we had our home. My father helped in the church and with forest firefighting crews and did occasional mail deliveries around the mountains. My mother was a nurse and midwife who ran the local clinic. She sometimes took me with her on visits to remote mountain cabins to bring medical care to isolated families. Her skills and dedication saved the lives of both people and animals, and ushered hundreds of babies into this life.

There were no veterinarians anywhere in the regions of those mountains in the 1950s. My mother's skill in stitching up wounded humans was occasionally called upon to help animals. One day, a man in deep distress came to the clinic in which we lived and pleaded with my mother to come with him to the mountain, where his logging mule lay mortally wounded after a rolling log wrapped a chain around its leg, tearing into the hind quarter muscles. My mother protested that she knew nothing about sewing up a mule, but he told her he didn't care. The mule was the only thing keeping his family from destitution. Without his mule, he could see no future, and he wanted her to try to save its life. If she couldn't, that was God's will, but to not try was unforgiveable. She took all the sulfa powder in the clinic, all the bandages and tape, all the sewing implements and supplies, everything that she had on hand, and rode with him in the truck to the place where the wounded mule lay on the mountainside. She walked up the steep terrain and while the men held the mule still, she worked for hours, kneeling on the forest floor, pouring the sulfa into the wound, and cleaning and stitching until she had done what she could do. The mule lived, much to her amazement.

The years in Arkansas established central themes in my life: the attachment problems, the striving for recognition and accomplishment, the fierce independence and outspokenness that often got me into trouble. It also grounded my passion for justice, fairness, and service, and motivated me to join with people that the dominant society ignores or discards.

I move easily in the borderlands, just like both of my parents...and just like Herb.

Probably the most formative early event of my life was getting lost as a toddler deep in the Ozark National Forest where the mission was located. It remains a miracle that I was ever found by searchers with tracker dogs. I've wondered in recent years: whose ancestral spirits watched over the lost child in the forest? Did birds and small animals come to me? Was I frightened or comforted? I remember the little bug I was following into the forest to see where it lived—and then everything goes dark. The memory disappears. I have come to understand now that there was a darkness of a more ominous nature that drew me into the forest, intending me harm, but forces of love stayed with me and kept me safe.

I remember other things from those very early days, such as being in my crib at night by the open window, clinging to the railing while peering at the stars and moon in the big night sky above the mountain behind the house. The nighttime calls and songs of the whippoorwills still echo in my memory with an essence of entranced wonder and awe.

I remember my pet chicken and the playhouse built by my father from corn shocks in the garden, and the dark, earthy smell of its cozy space inside. I remember the flood that destroyed the peanuts and watermelons I had planted by myself, and the bitter tears I shed when I saw the flooded garden. I remember my pet dogs and cats and the hours of joy playing with them. There were few opportunities to play with other children, except when going to the tiny church twice on Sunday and once on Wednesday night. Behaving and being quiet in church was an impossibility for my enthusiastic child nature, and I remember my mother's sternness. The gurgling stream that ran by the house and church called to me, and I played there for hours, searching for tiny stones and frogs and crayfish and minnows. Nature was my teacher, and my pet dog was my protector companion who comforted me in a loneliness that went DNA deep.

When I was born, my parents loved me dearly but hardly knew what to do with me. They were in their late thirties and I was their first baby. I slept little and cried much, confounding the limits of their patience, and I ended up being abused as a result of my mother's frustrated, frayed, nervous determination to make me be "a good girl." My mystified father indulged me generously, and he often argued loudly and bitterly with my mother over their differences in raising a child like me. Those early frightening arguments formed my opinion of myself as a problem, someone who was deeply flawed, needing to fix everyone and everything so the world could be a safe place, but who would fail miserably at ever succeeding.

The happiest event of my early childhood was the birth of a baby brother the month before I turned three—an event that came a day after I had disappeared, again. When found, a mile up the creek with not a stitch of clothing anywhere, I was beaten by my mother to teach me not to "run away." The hardest thing in my early years was never knowing or understanding when or why the harsh punishment "teaching" would be applied. I lived with fear much of the time, while also having loving attention from both parents and others the rest of the time. I just never knew or could predict which it was going to be, when I was going to be coddled or beaten, and fear formed my psyche. Strange lessons to try to integrate into a child's soul when Sunday School teaches that Jesus loves you and would want you to turn the other cheek to violence and be peaceful. I experienced the unfairness of violence and could not cope with what I now know was the resulting cognitive dissonance. Dissociation became part of my psychological makeup, creating difficulties for me throughout my life.

When I was entering the second grade, a year younger than everyone else in the class—because my parents sent me to school early to get me out from underfoot—my family moved to Pennsylvania, which they called "home." The mission board had closed the Arkansas clinic and my mother, grieving the loss of her missionary status and her professional independence in the clinic, was forced to go to work in a hospital to keep her career, a circumstance that she both hated and loved. She was always torn between her family strivings and her desires for a medical career. She always seemed exhausted to me after the move to Pennsylvania. It seemed to me that she seldom smiled or laughed again.

Looking back on my memories from that time in my life, I am still filled with sadness at the trauma I experienced as a little child who could not understand why my favourite old toys and treasured, worn doll "Susy" had to be tossed on the big fire used to get rid of unwanted household items when my parents packed their belongings to move. I remember sobbing uncontrollably as I looked out the rear car window, watching my beloved pet dog throwing himself against his chain, barking wildly as we drove away. My mother explained he would be cared for by his new family. My father's silence told me his heart was also breaking.

My maternal grandparent's farm was our new home in the countryside near the small town of Willow Street, Pennsylvania, just on the edge of William Penn's land grant in the traditional territory of the Susquehannock nation. My father's Mennonite family had fallen apart when he was a child, but his foster family, who were Old Order Mennonites, cared for him. As his second family, they warmly welcomed us also. His sisters and their families rounded out the new constellation of the circle of my life. There were so many new things, and adaptation was made more difficult with the sadness and somberness of the adults around me.

After living on the farm for almost a year, we moved into town so that my mother's drive to work at the hospital in the city would not be so far. I was thrust into yet another new world, unlike anything I had ever known before. I was the strangely dressed, tiny Mennonite girl in a huge public school, dealing daily with more children than I had ever known existed. The adults were bizarre in my frame of reference, and I often didn't understand what they were saying, or what they expected of me. The school bus was frightening, the bullying children more so, and it felt like my brain was shutting down. I was told that I talked like an "Okie" (a slur toward a certain southern US dialect), and that I looked like someone in a pioneer picture. I was smaller and younger than my classmates and completely ignorant of the clothes, games, dances, jewelry, and television shows familiar to them. There was no place to hide. There was only daydreaming, getting lost in my imagination, and dissociation. What used to be so easy in school became impossibly difficult—the nightmares became worse, and the temper tantrums more so. Our family thrived on misery in those early years in Pennsylvania.

By the time high school came around, another brother had been added to the family. He was almost 10 years younger than me, one for whom I was given a great deal of responsibility. During that time, my father's mother came to live with us, following the closure of the Pennsylvania State Psychiatric Hospital. The symptoms of her mental illness dominated our family interactions. The stress of it all as my mother struggled to cope with her care, and the care of three children along with a full-time nursing job, was indescribable. I sometimes wonder how it was that we children were never removed from our home. Eventually, Grandma went to live at the Lancaster County Home where we visited her weekly. Those visits were painful for all of us in various ways, but processes of resilience and adaptation, built into the network of our Mennonite culture, served to provide what we needed to survive in the face of the difficulties and ambiguities of living with the impact of a family member's mental illness. I think my father suffered more than I could have ever realized as a child.

My parents sent me to Lancaster Mennonite High School when I was 13 years old, where I truly began to thrive and the world began to open up for me. I was immersed in an environment that fit with my family's culture. In high school, I was surprised to discover I was smart. Until then, I had believed I was stupid and lazy—sentiments gathered as a result of my experiences in public school along with my mother's unpredictable and rageful outbursts. I now understand those episodes as her plea for help, expressing how she felt about herself and her life and not a pronouncement of my true self, but a child cannot fully understand these things.

My mother was a gifted, wounded healer, trapped in a life that stifled her spirit. My father struggled with job insecurity but eventually went back to school and became an X-Ray technician, which relieved some of our family's financial distress, and, I think, raised our collective self-esteem. I felt so proud of my father, knowing he got A's in his classes, and I was especially impressed with his big physics textbook.

Singing in the school choir opened doors to a life with joy and social opportunities for me. My parents were now able to take the family on summer vacations, and send us to summer camp, and we all had piano lessons after they purchased an old upright piano. I got my first jobs babysitting and working in restaurants. My teen years, for the first time, brought me close friends, adventures, freedom from the confines and conflicts at home, and the life of my extended family seemed a bit happier as well. Hope flourished for my future, yet the shadows remained, and the struggle for internal distance and external connections built a force like trapped steam in my soul, contributing to a deep inner split in my heart. The world was a place of desire, a place of fear, and I had scant light for the path to find my way in it.

Old friends know additional layers of my story from the days of our undergraduate studies at Goshen College, a Mennonite undergraduate school in the prairie region of northern Indiana on traditional Potawatomi territory. It was not too far from Chicago, but far enough to deter many trips to the big city attractions of worldly temptations. In my case, the deterrence wasn't strong enough to halt my exit from the close-knit Mennonite world, an egress that had begun in my early development and been further nurtured in my late adolescence. My ambivalent departure had in it the seeds of the Arkansas childhood. I lived a double life, and the hints of that deeply distressed my family.

By the time I was in my late twenties, I was married to my college sweetheart, living in Toledo, Ohio, where he was completing medical training and I was completing a Master of Social Work degree at the University of Michigan, an hour's drive from our Toledo apartment. No one who knew me in that world comprehended where I had come from, how far I had stretched to arrive in the career of a young professional married to a doctor, preparing to enter a realm of privilege from a formerly marginal existence. I longed to be accepted in the mainstream, and all my strivings focused on that direction. There were many ways to hide there, but I had only a small frame of reference to decorate and twist into a semblance of solid validity.

Keeping my "Okie"/Mennonite heritage as secret as possible seemed a necessary step for my new life as a doctor's wife, and for many years I hid my origins, and much of my life, from most people who knew me. Living a far distance from my family helped. The many manifestations of that internal split took its toll on my sense of self, my identity, my relationships, and my ability to be a whole person. It took until my marriage to Herb for me to fully integrate myself, embrace my identity, and begin to heal some of the cultural and historical wounds I carried.

At 29, I was soon to welcome my first daughter into the world. It was a time of intense ups and downs. "Well, *that* happened," a new friend said to me recently as we exchanged stories of our lives. We were laughing together, sharing the realization that some of the best things we've ever done have been in times of terrible challenge and difficulty. Mistakes pile upon one another and soon the bandages accrue, unable to hold the framework together. Many things happened to lead me and my husband off course, away from a shared life together.

ॐ

After the birth of my second daughter while living in the Appalachian Regional Commission area in southern Ohio, our little family moved to the shores of the Mississippi River in southern Iowa. This was Ioway, and Sauk and Fox traditional territory, close to the final winter camp of Black Hawk, the great Sauk leader who died of old age in Iowa in 1838. All his brave efforts to stem the flow of settlers across the Mississippi River were for naught. His story interested me. I began to research it and wrote an article about him published in *The Muzzleloader* magazine. It was while living in Iowa that I became serious about writing and experienced some small success.

Our new home was at a place where the great Mississippi River flows from east to west as it turns between the states of Illinois, Iowa, and Missouri before rolling down toward the far distance into the Gulf of Mexico. It's a location rich in history, and with my interest in history, I soon became involved in the activities of the reconstructed Old Fort Madison in my new town. In addition to continuing my career as a clinical social worker, I served on the city commission that operated the Old Fort as a tourist attraction, helping to create a unique living history museum on the shores of the Mississippi River. The Old Fort leadership strove to portray the story of both the Indigenous peoples of the region and the settlers that came with the expanding boundaries of the United States.

On the shores of the Mississippi River, I met my first traditional teacher, Wayne Medicine Eagle Hagmeier, who with many friends helped lead the work of creating the Old Fort historical site. Wayne was a Renaissance man in many ways, a self-educated person sought out by state archaeologists whenever a consultant was needed on Native American sites. He was an artist, and his reproduction artifacts were placed in museums to facilitate the return of the original piece to the people it belonged to, or to be archived appropriately. He both consulted on and acted in movies that portrayed the life of the regional Indigenous peoples, but more importantly, Wayne was a Medicine Man, trained by a Lakota Elder for over 30 years even though he was of Ioway and German descent.

I was in my mid-thirties when Wayne began to teach me the meaning of the Sacred Medicines and introduced me to the traditional Lakota "purification lodge." He spent hours sharing teachings with me and introducing me to people of various Native American nations and Canadian First Nations whom he knew. I went with him and some of these friends to my first Pow Wows and started learning some drum songs and dances. It was Wayne who came to my home and conducted a cleansing ceremony after my husband filed for divorce.

The end of my life as I knew it began with the break-up of my family, which propelled me into many years of confused and troubled attempts to regain a new balance. I made mistakes over and over in those years, but Wayne's example of how imperfect people can still move towards spiritual health and work to improve their lives was a priceless gift to me.

The new name Wayne gave to me, Red Hawk Woman, inspired and comforted me as I moved into a new life, one which few of my family and friends could understand. My special connection with the Red Tail Hawk was sacred to me, and Wayne's recognition of that was helpful. I struggled a great deal for over seven years before I began to feel that I was putting some of my troubles behind me. My daughters managed to survive the struggles, due in large part to their own wonderful strengths and spiritual gifts, but also due to the resilient nature of love's processes. We moved back to Goshen, Indiana, and I attempted to start life over.

When Wayne died in 2001, my daughters and I travelled back to Iowa for his funeral, conducted with both traditional Lakota ceremonies and with military honours since he was a veteran. The journey to say goodbye to such an important person in our lives left us raw with grief. Wayne's life had a big impact on us. He and his wife, Dee, brought much fun and enrichment to our lives, and it took a long time to integrate the reality of his loss.

Dee later went on to sponsor Pow Wows in his memory and committed to working at a Sun Dance in his memory for four consecutive years. In 2003, for her third Sun Dance, she needed a driver to get from Iowa to South Dakota, so I volunteered. It was a pivotal event in my life, a fulcrum for the many dramatic changes that have taken place since then.

On the Rosebud Reservation at the Sun Dance, I had the unusual experience of spending the majority of the time in the Moon Camp. I was going through the menopause transition that all women experience later in life and unexpectedly began my "moon time" (menstruation), which meant I could not be around the ceremonial site. It was a gift of rich alone time. Later, a teenage girl arrived at the Moon Camp, heartbroken at having to sit out the dance. She was a supporter for her father, one of the Sun Dancers, and finding herself experiencing the sacred time in Moon Camp because of her "moon time" saddened her. It was only the two of us as we talked about teachings of the gift and power of this sacred time, and spent hours walking across the many miles of freedom that being in Moon Camp provided. We ate the food that was brought and served to us, slept in the tent, and sat on a hill with an ancient stone circle above the Sun Dance grounds, and together we watched birds soar and prairie dogs scamper about. As we shared stories, she poured out her grief about her mother's murder in front of her when she was just a little girl.

When the Sun Dancers had completed their ceremony, we returned to the main camp for the feasts and celebrations, and I spent the evening with her and the family going over things we had talked about in our solitary experience. These conversations were the beginning of a great healing in their family. I have seldom felt so clearly guided by Creator, so deeply involved in a healing process. It confirmed for me that I could trust myself with the guidance of Creator in my life. The reasons why I had experienced certain things, and why I had been invited to that particular Sun Dance, became clearer. Other sacred things came to me during that time also, initiating me into a new shape for my life and beginning the trajectory of my path to a loving Ojibway family in northern Ontario, married to a man who would bring so much healing to my own mother, children, and siblings.

THE MYSTERY OF MOTHER

How did that little Mennonite girl get from the southern mountain forests to a grown-up life with Herb Nabigon, Oji-Cree Elder, living out his final years on the northern shore of Lake Superior in Ontario, Canada? Two such very different people were unlikely to ever meet, let alone make a life together and create an ordinary, happy marriage. Even now I'm not sure I can fully unpack all the mysteries of that journey through my life. The farther back in history I go to try to unravel all the threads, the more complicated it becomes, even as light is shed on the pieces and parts of my ancestry and my story.

The biggest mystery is the relationship with my mother, one that Herb tried to help me better understand early on in our marriage. The more research I did on my ancestry, the more I tried to make sense of my mother's life, and thus my own. It's an ongoing endeavor, but in a strange way, my knowledge that death does not end a relationship has helped, and my relationship with my mother has improved over the years since her passing. My edges have softened, my heart has opened, but trying to understand the mystery of my mother seems to be a life-long theme for me. Herb understood that. He could relate because his experience with his mother's death when he was a young teenager took many decades to heal. I'm still always trying to figure out yet another layer of gratitude and pain, all mixed together. Maybe if I could time-travel back into deep, ancient history, I could find the source of all the trouble.

Mom did not want me to get remarried as it went against her religious beliefs, but when she saw I was determined, she told me, "Make sure you can get a job up there in Canada, and make sure you listen to your husband," instructions that reflected both her modern feminist leanings and her old-fashioned traditional values.

She welcomed Herb into her home when we went to visit her after our wedding in 2006. They had met briefly a few months earlier at my brother's home in International Falls, Minnesota, but when Herb came to her home, my mother really opened up to him and started treating him like a son. He responded with kindness and dignity, respecting her as a son respects a treasured parent. She showed him the large, old family Bible and opened her cedar chest to show us the dress she wanted to be buried in. While we were talking, Herb shared with her that he lived with the illness of diabetes, and she immediately went into "nurse mode." She wanted to look at his feet. Good-natured Herb took off his shoes, and the two of them put their heads together, looking at his feet and talking about foot care. She exhorted him to always be sure to change his socks.

Later, we chuckled together about the day's events, and Herb said something to me that went to my heart. He said, "Always listen to the elders. Show respect for them and never argue with them. Just agree with whatever they say, and if you don't follow what they say, well don't worry about it. Just don't be surprised. They have a lot of wisdom. That's what our people have always taught. Listen to the elders!" I told him that if he understood my mother's cantankerous ways it would be a way to understand me better, but I would try to stop arguing with her.

Having grown up learning to follow my mother's example and arguing with her whenever I disagreed, I felt ashamed. How had I been so wrong about my mother? I began to realize over the years ahead that Herb was right. Arguing with her was never productive and just made us both miserable. But I had only five years after our marriage in 2006 to try to take a different approach in dealing with my difficult mother.

At the age of 95, she had been living independently, raging about no longer being allowed to drive, reluctantly giving over the task of laundry to someone else. And then came the fall, outside her home on an icy driveway as she bent to retrieve her Wednesday morning newspaper. I travelled through a deep winter snowstorm from Ontario to Pennsylvania, and spent time sitting beside her in the hospital, waiting for hip surgery to be scheduled, frustrated that it was taking so long. I tried to imagine a 96th birthday party in an assisted living facility, a skilled surgeon who could halt her slide into rapid decline, thinking we would still have time to learn to love each other, or at least forgive each other. We were not the "quiet in the land"—*die stille im lande,* as Mennonites were once known. Our contest had waxed and waned throughout my entire life, yet we were careful now with our hard-won détente.

Now we were partners in the endeavors of keeping the pillow placed just right and the angle of her leg just so in order that the pain could be tolerated. She was restless, looking out the window, or at the door, wondering aloud, "Am I being good?" I turned away to hide my tears, hating all that had happened to her to make that a pressing question while awaiting surgery. I read aloud her favorite Psalms from her Bible as she lay on the hospital bed, agitated and uncomfortable, until the dose of Haldol was increased and she slept more restfully, but also seemed less lucid. She had lived a difficult life, which she was struggling with yet again as she came to terms with the hated immobility.

As long as I could remember, my mother and I had circled each other like wary competitors, both mystified as to what the competition was all about. In the last three months of her life, I believe she sought to relax and let go of the anxiety that had driven her, and driven me away from her. As a child, my name for her was Mama, but later, it became Mom and never changed. I think saying Mama felt too close to her fierce, controlling, possessive love, and saying Mom was a way to set a boundary, to put a safe distance between us, pushing us apart, pulling us together. She called her own mother Mama all her life, and at the end of her life, she spoke poignantly of memories of her loved and revered Mama and Papa, as if they had only passed away a few years prior.

My mother had spent many years in hospitals as a nurse-midwife. Her training was at the Pennsylvania Hospital School of Nursing during World War II, where she saw the early experimentation of penicillin on patients being tested by the U.S. War Board. As a student on her surgical rotation, she was a minor assistant for the first hip replacement performed in the U.S. When I told the surgeon about her experiences as he consulted with her on the plans for the surgery, he began to speak to her differently. He made eye contact with her, and his tone seemed more respectful, but I noticed he had difficulty looking at me as he left her room. I thought the expression on his face was one of embarrassment. Did he know that I had sensed his initial disregard of her, or perhaps had he sensed my irritation at him for what I perceived to be a dismissal of a non-descript, tiny old woman? *She could have taught him a few things*, I thought.

My mother and I had time to talk in moments when she was feeling better. It had been many years since we had shared quiet time, to simply be in each other's presence without agendas or schedules. Those were the tools of our protection, for ourselves and each other. I had questions that I wanted to hear her answer, although she had probably answered them long ago.

"Why did Grandpa and Grandma not let you go to high school?" I asked. "Was it just because the church said it was wrong?"

Perhaps due to the discomfort of confinement, her reply came in that grumpy tone of voice I remembered so well from childhood, sending the usual cringe into my shoulders and neck. "There wasn't any high school in our area, and there was no way for me to get to the city, and no money to pay for it. Back then, if you didn't live in the city, you had to pay. I was the oldest and they needed me to work on the farm." This would have been in the years of the Great Depression. Just weeks prior to the banks in Lancaster, Pennsylvania closing, my grandfather withdrew all the money he had been saving for over ten years and put it towards the purchase of a small, 60-acre farm with two houses, a barn, and a large tobacco shed built into the side of a hill that had a chicken house in its lower level. Eventually, they added a cement-block summer kitchen behind the big, red-brick farmhouse. Rental income from the second house helped to pay bills.

In spring and summer, my mother's younger brothers and sisters gathered flowers from the woodland and fields the day before Saturday's trip to the city market. Meanwhile, she helped my grandmother bake the loaves of bread they would take to sell, along with vegetables from the truck patch and leftover eggs that the family could do without. Leaving in pre-dawn darkness for the hours-long trip in a horse-drawn farm wagon, they dozed, or talked together about their anticipations of the day. While their parents sold food at the market, the children walked the streets selling "posies for a penny," and sometimes were allowed to buy some candy before the return trip home.

Mom did eventually get her coveted high school diploma. In 1937, she saw a small advertisement in the newspaper for high school by correspondence, and secretly enrolled. When the courses began arriving in the mail, she told her parents she intended to complete her education now that she was "21 and legal" and had her own money. As long as she did her farm work, there wasn't much they could say.

After many years of working so hard during the day and studying late into the night, my mother exploded in rage at her father, demanding that she be allowed to sleep in the morning and not be expected to rise at 4:00 AM to milk the cows. He had given each of her three younger brothers money to get married and start their own lives, and the unfairness of her life chipped away at her ability to "be a good girl." Grandpa relented about the early milking, and Mom never again had to deal with smelly cows in the morning darkness. She also never had much time for a social life in those years and became isolated, though still embedded in her close-knit Mennonite community. Life was about family, farm, and church, and by studying in all her free time, my mother placed herself apart. I think the loneliness that stemmed from those years was at the core of a deep hurt in her heart, unassuaged by faith or career, husband or children. Her infectious grief, expressed in anger, was passed on to us all—my younger brothers, my father, and me—and none of us understood until it was too late.

When Mom's last high school correspondence course arrived, it was the chemistry class she had been putting off as long as she could. Without a chemistry credit she could not get the diploma she had worked for, so hard and so long. The problem was the lab requirement. There was still no way to get to the school in the city. Grandpa only took the horse and wagon there on market day. Somehow my mother persuaded the mail carrier to give her a ride in the mail truck, sitting on the bags of mail for the trip to the city, where she worked and studied in the chemistry lab at McCaskey High School one day a week. At the end of the day, she got the mail truck back to the country farm. It's hard to imagine what it must have been like for her, a tiny, conservative Mennonite woman in her 20s, to face down strange looks and whispers from city teenagers on those excruciating days in a big city school where she "stuck out like a sore thumb," as she said to me when telling the story.

As soon as she had her diploma in hand, my mother applied to and was accepted by the prestigious Pennsylvania School of Nursing in Philadelphia during the years when World War II raged around the globe. She graduated the year after the war ended. Her amazing career as a nurse-midwife began as a result of a war in which Mennonites did not take up arms, but instead saw thousands of their young men (including my father) go off to regions around the United States to serve for years in the Civilian Public Service. World War II was the hammer that broke open the shell around an insulated Mennonite world existing on this continent since their exodus from the violence directed at them in Europe in the 1600's and 1700's. As a result, Mom was able to obtain the coveted R.N. degree and eventually a Bachelor of Arts from Goshen College, where she wrote a small history book about her community *Out of the Silent Past* (by Rhoda Campbell), still sometimes referenced today by historians of the Pennsylvania Mennonites.

Three months after the fall, Mom's heart stopped. The family and her community met together for her funeral at the church some of her ancestors had helped build 300 years before, when they were newly arrived settlers having escaped the genocide of Mennonites in Europe. The farm fields, long cleared of ancient, giant trees, still clung to the rolling terrain surrounding the cemetery where we gathered on an unseasonably warm and bright mid-March day to share our final words. My youngest brother, the Mennonite minister, said his own words and prayers. I did not want to be there. I did not want to see her plain, pine casket, crafted by an Amish carpenter, lowered into the deep darkness of the damp grave. I woke in the early morning hours for many nights later, oppressed by the thought of my mother's body lying in that cold, dark place, remembering how we took our turns with shovels to fill her grave, as is the old custom in Mennonite burials.

In those conversations shared at the end of her life, weaving back and forth from childhood to her more recent years, consolidating all her gains, reviewing so much that she needed to remember, I saw how reminiscing became the most important work Mom ever did. I said, "You've worked so hard, all your life," and I held her hand and listened. I said to her, "I love you, I thank you, I forgive you. Will you forgive me?"

She replied with a tender touch of her frail hand to my cheek. "Oh, Annie, there's nothing to forgive. It was always about love." It was strong emotional work, and I think if I can hold on to that as long as I can remember, I will find my own way to a deeper wholeness.

Herb did not attend my mother's funeral. He did not like funerals. Later, he expressed regret that he hadn't been there, but I understood. His own mother's death had deeply impacted his life, and I had no desire to force an experience on him that would tear open those bitter old wounds. It seemed easier for me to keep this part of my life separate from him, as so much of his life was separate from mine.

Years later, we went to her grave together, and he did a Pipe Ceremony, and we prayed. We walked for a while among the grave markers as I pointed out the names of my ancestors, and then we drove past the farm where I had lived briefly in my childhood after Arkansas. We did not stop. I did not want to disturb the Amish family living there. They would have recognized me because I had visited once before with Dorothy, Herb's sister, but now was not a time for a visit. Herb and I were both in a reflective mood.

We mused together on what the land might have looked like before the settlers came, and we drove across the bridge over the Conestoga River. I told him the story of the Conestoga people, a remnant of the Susquehannock Nation, and the final genocide that had taken place in Lancaster in 1763. It would be some years later that we learned of the role some of my Campbell ancestors had in events leading up to the tragedy. My mother's father's people had come from Scotland and Ireland, not the Mennonite diaspora of Germany and Switzerland. Although I can find no evidence of any direct ancestor participating in the killing (and I have searched extensively), all of my Mother's ancestors were squatters on land that was known back then as the "Conestoga Manor," reserved for the Conestoga people and "legalized" by a written treaty signed by William Penn.

My father's ancestors settled in a different part of Lancaster County during colonization. All of my ancestors were settlers on territory where they had no true rights to live, and they colluded with, or turned a blind eye to, those who "disappeared" the Indigenous peoples of the region. For the most part, Mennonite people, like other settler descendants, have little comprehension of the genocide committed against the Indigenous peoples of North America. There is no comprehension of the crimes they participated in, which included some Mennonite farmers in the Carlisle, Pennsylvania area, keeping Indigenous children as farm laborers, their services purchased from the Carlisle Indian School there during the 1800s. To this day there is no public apology from the larger Mennonite Church organizational leadership regarding the privileges gained from the genocide, although some congregations in some areas have acknowledged and apologized.

It is a bitter knowledge. The story of the Conestoga people was a hard one for Herb and me to navigate. It doesn't help to know that two Conestoga survivors, an elderly husband and wife, lived out their lives under the protection of a Mennonite family. It only complicates the processing of a painful subject. It doesn't help to remember that my grandfather was the first Campbell, to my knowledge, to embrace pacifism—I know his ancestors, my ancestors, truly carried hatred in their hearts for the First Peoples. I'm still working this out, turning it over in my mind, praying for healing.

My Mennonite ancestors, though, carry a deeper puzzle for me. Did they join the settler life for freedom? For safety? Were they economic refugees, or opportunistic land hunters duped by the colonizers? Some, or all of the above? I do not know the answers to those questions. I do know that they came with firm beliefs in non-violence, non-participation in government but obedience to it, strong values of separation of church and state, and a determination to be left alone, separate from "the world" but serving others as a way to serve God. Those core values have shaped my life, but Mennonites now are more assimilated into the world around them. They aren't the same people I left so many decades ago. I can never visit that place of my mother's grave without sensing the pain and grief of the displaced Indigenous peoples, layered with the woundedness of my ancestors.

On May 18, 2013, Herb and I attended the opening dedication of the Longhouse at the Hans Herr House Museum in Willow Street, Pennsylvania, not far from where my mother had lived in her early childhood. Herb was there to introduce himself in *Anishnaabemowin*, his mother tongue, and was among representatives of over 30 different Indigenous nations in attendance. He had a little table set up to sell his book, but not many people were in the mood to buy, which deeply disappointed him. I think there were many disappointments for Herb in that visit, but his spirits improved when he met a white man who spoke his language and they conversed together. Later that evening, we had a sacred fire at my brother's home and he smudged and did a teaching as he shared his Pipe with our family. It is a good memory, that final visit to

Lancaster which Herb and I made together.

When I go back now, alone, to see my mother and father's graves, side by side, and look out across the gentle rolling farm fields around the old church, there is a wash of memories flooding across my mind, and I feel close to Herb there, as I do to my ancestors and the spirits of the original people. I say a prayer for all our peoples, past and present, and hold up my hopes for Creator to bless us all. I hold my hopes for peace and reconciliation in my heart.

What was once here cannot be brought back, just as Herb's body is gone and cannot be restored to me, to his family, to life. I must go on, build my own life again, and what is to come can be built in a good way. Likewise, settler descendants and Indigenous peoples can go on together to build *Minobimadiziwin,* a good life, if we respect the traditions and share Mother Earth with love, respect, and kindness. Herb firmly believed in *minobimadiziwin,* and it's what he worked for—for the healing of his people.

We need to respect our elders and their teachings and learn from past mistakes. My mitochondrial DNA tests tell me that, deeper into history, my remote ancestors travelled across the continents from Africa to Europe, ending up in the high mountains of Switzerland, the river valleys and fields of Germany, and the lovely moors of Scotland. When my ancestors crossed the waters to this continent, it was life and safety they sought, and the ignorance and greed carried with them is not unlike the ignorance and greed that plagues any human society, especially the modern society we live in today. But there is also sharing and generosity, love and forgiveness, strength and hope. Just as the Medicine Wheel portrays the duality of positive and negative, there is an embedded wholeness and reciprocity in life, which is activated by love and respect. We have Elders far more ancient than could be imagined in the light of day. They are waiting to give us guidance. All this has come to me through my mother, and my mother's mother, and so on in an unbroken line back into time immemorial, a time that is a mystery to us now. It has also come to me from the traditions of the Indigenous family Herb brought me into, whose lives I have joined with mine.

As Herb said, we have to respect our elders—it's the only way to shed enough light on the path.

A Meeting with the Teachings

It might be easier to follow the weavings of this story I am trying to tell if I share a bit of the background of how the traditional teachings began to guide the life I lived with Herb. From the beginning, he instructed me in the teachings that gave meaning to his life and brought healing to his heart.

Not too long after we met, Herb sent me a publisher's galley copy of his book, *The Hollow Tree: Fighting Addiction with Traditional Native Healing.* He wanted me to learn about his worldview and spiritual understandings. The question of what I myself thought I needed to learn was not fully formed in my mind. It was not the question I was asking myself. I was just aware that there were things he wanted me to know so I set about trying to learn his ways.

I read over and over the chapters on the Four Sacred Directions, The Hub, The Medicine Wheel, and the fascinating story of his life. To help me remember, I drew my own little sketch of the teachings of the Medicine Wheel and taped it to the back of my apartment door. Each day as I headed for work, I faced the door, ready to embark on another day, and reviewed the sketch hoping for the words and meaning to penetrate enough for me to recall later. It wasn't easy for me to memorize things after my head injury, but making a drawing of my own helped me anchor new information. Each time I touched the doorknob I made a connection in my brain to the Medicine Wheel. The knowledge slowly began to generalize into my life as I integrated a new way of thinking into my daily routines.

My way of learning is visual and kinesthetic, not through hearing but through seeing and experiencing. Since my accident in 2003, I have trouble with short-term memory and rely on writing things down, making drawings, and repetition to try to get things into long-term memory. The original teachings Herb shared in his book came from a time when the culture was based in oral transmission of knowledge, as well as through art and ceremony. People absorbed all that they knew from hearing traditional teachings and living in the traditional ways. I learn from oral teachings by creating visualizations in my mind and drawing or writing what I'm hearing. Living out what I learn anchors the wisdom given to me.

The reciprocity of learning from a life connected with the land, integrating the intricate understandings of Indigenous knowledge, is something that people around the planet now need to relearn since colonization destroyed most ancient oral traditions. Herb was trained in the traditional teachings, in the "Old Way," and what he knew he gained from his own personal experience growing up in the bush as a child, and later working to heal himself. His mainstream education and role as a university professor made it possible for him to find ways to braid together ancient knowledge and wisdom with new ways. He helped many people through his writings and teachings where he incorporated both the traditional knowledge sharing and the mainstream methods of teaching.

I began to bring my new understandings into the group therapy I was doing at the mental health clinic where I worked, in which we used a cognitive behavioural, strengths-based approach in the structure of the therapy process (known as CBT). I discovered that my clients really enjoyed putting things into the shape of a circle and could make more sense of the CBT strategies I was trying to teach them by connecting things to a direction and a color. Sometimes we drew our own circles and wrote things down or passed around a copy of the Medicine Wheel drawing I was working on. I began to share on a more spiritual level. Sharing by group members got more personal and real. People opened up more easily and began to connect with each other strongly. I was amazed at the power of the Medicine Wheel teachings to bring healing to the lives of people struggling to live with the effects of severe mental illness.

Later, while working on my doctoral studies, Herb and I authored an article together about ways to braid traditional healing with mainstream approaches to therapy. We described a way to bring the teachings into real life situations, maintaining respect and acknowledgement of the origins of the traditions. At the heart of the work is the acknowledgement of Spirit, and the ability of Spirit to help people with open hearts who are ready to do the work. Without this recognition of reciprocity and acknowledgement, the traditions are empty. Without the connection to Spirit, true healing cannot happen in a lasting way, and the knowledge is nothing more than hollow ritual.

"No one owns Spirit," Herb used to say. "It cannot be bought and should not be used in a bad way." I heard him say many times, "The longest journey is from the head to the heart." I trusted he knew what he was talking about from personal experience, which is the only way to approach Spirit. We can't separate the heart and the mind if we want to find wholeness.

In the process of doing my work I began to do more research on the Medicine Wheel. Eventually, I came up with a drawing as a symbol to recall important teachings and lessons. The knowledge has been shared with me, passed on to me by Herb Nabigon the Elder, but he was also my husband, and this knowledge was very personal to us, not to be appropriated.

The Medicine Wheel

Spiritual

North Door

White
Winter
Caucasians
Air
Elders

Movement
Sweet Grass
Strength
Caring
Bear
(Non-Caring)

West Door

Black
Autumn
African Peoples
Water
Reasoning

Sage
Adults
Respect
Thunderbird
(Resentment)

Mother Earth

East Door

Red
Spring
Indigenous Peoples
Food
Childhood

Vision
Tobacco
Kindness
Turtle
(Inferiority)

South Door

Yellow
Summer
Asians
Earth
Golden Eagle

Patience
Time
Youth
Cedar
Relationships
(Envy)

Intellectual

Emotional

Physical

The Seven Wisdom (Grandfather) Teachings:
Love, Bravery, Wisdom, Honesty, Humility, Truth, Respect

The Rascals
Non-Caring, Inferiority, Envy, Resentment, Jealousy

(From: Herb Nabigon, *The Hollow Tree: Fighting Addiction with Traditional Native Healing,* 2006; and personal conversations)

Herb could easily talk extemporaneously on each word written here and take days to cover it all. I do not carry that much knowledge within me, but when I sit and reflect on this page, which I often do, I am able to recall many of his teachings and remember the essential aspects I have written down.

He had so deeply integrated these teachings into his ways of living that most of the time it went without saying. I would know what he was thinking about from just a few words, such as, "The rascals are at it again." This was one of our little inside phrases to indicate that the duality of the Medicine Wheel teachings was asserting some truth from within the shadow side. There were feelings being activated that were troublesome. Herb acknowledged that when the rascals are working, we need to respect them inside of ourselves, not judge or condemn, but take responsibility and work to improve a situation.

This is just one example of how we used traditional teachings in very practical ways in our life together. Mostly, though, we did not directly talk about the Medicine Wheel, or other traditional teachings, even though they formed the framework for our daily interactions. We had other things we practiced too, from time to time, such as smudging with sage or sweetgrass, praying with the Pipe, walking in nature, sitting by a sacred fire, or putting tobacco down by a tree or in the water. These were simple reminders of the natural reciprocity necessary for every aspect of life with the Spirit and were an integral part of our daily lives.

The traditions are multifaceted, unique to each Nation, and are taught in a variety of ways by people who come from many different directions. Herb could only share what was given to him from the Oji-Cree traditions, and he made them his own. He used to say, "It doesn't become your own until you use it in your life and pass it on." I'm grateful for the time we had together, that I have something I have made my own, and that he taught me to pass it on.

THE EAST DOOR

VISION

The late October evening darkened early, and as I rushed from my office to the car, I noticed how the wind seemed to bend the trees as if determined to shake the last dry leaves to the ground. Deep purple clouds threatening rain raced low over the city of Fort Wayne, Indiana, as I drove through the usual after-work traffic, frustrated by long lines of cars and delays at the lights. I remembered another evening like this one just a little over two years before and shivered, having a sudden flashback to the sounds of screeching tires, and breaking glass. I took a few deep breaths and focused on relaxing. "No more accidents," I whispered to myself. "No need to rush."

Before I left my apartment that morning, I had carefully placed everything in the car that I would need for the events of the evening, so there was no need to stop at home before heading out into the countryside to John and Beth Beam's farm. I was so eager for the Sweat Lodge ceremony. It had been a very long time since an opportunity presented itself to participate in the ceremony that had become an integral part of my life over the past ten years. I only needed to stop at the grocery store on the way out of town and pick up some food to share at the feast after our prayers in the Sweat Lodge. It would only take a minute. I could relax and slow down. There was plenty of time to get there by seven o'clock.

As I drove, slower, more relaxed, I let my mind wander over the memories of the previous two years. In September 2003, in this very city where I now lived, I was driving in the heavy rush hour traffic on Coliseum Boulevard to meet friends who lived in the city. Then, I'd been driving for over an hour, singing and praying as I went, and feeling good about how things were progressing in my life. Earlier that year, at the Sun Dance Ceremony in South Dakota, I experienced a profound shift in my consciousness. With new intentions, I returned to my home in Goshen,

Indiana, and proceeded to fulfill what I felt called to do. I gave my beloved mustang horse, Starr, to my brother, whose eight children would be better companions for the feisty little horse than a mostly absentee middle-aged woman who hardly ever rode. I divided my large house into upstairs and downstairs apartments and found a renter for the upstairs. I paid off many bills and made plans to expand my private counseling practice.

"Dear Creator," I prayed, "thank you so much for helping me meet my goals. Now all I need is to get rid of this car payment somehow. Please help me do that." Less than an hour later, Creator answered my heartfelt prayer, but not in any way I'd imagined, and the cascade of events that poured into my life with that answer resulted in an unusual and phenomenal transformation of my world.

There was only one problem. I had forgotten to add the caveat, "... with no harm coming to anyone."

As I sat at a red light in Fort Wayne, Indiana, that evening in 2003, I listened to the rain pound on the roof of my sporty little red car. I was the fourth vehicle back from the intersection, waiting for the light to change, when the answer to my prayer charged into my life. A large, dual-cab F350 Ford pick-up truck slammed into the back of my car so hard that the first car in line flew into the intersection.

When I regained consciousness, I realized that my head had hit the steering wheel and slammed back against the headrest before coming to rest on the steering wheel again. Blood was trickling from my nose, but I could not figure out what was the strange wetness on my face. I mopped it from my face with tissues and looked at the red colour, thinking, "blood." It surprised me for some reason. I felt no pain. I reached for my phone and called the friend I was meeting, leaving a message of where I was and asking her to come get me. I thought I had to figure out how to take care of myself and kept assuring the strangers at my car door that I was okay, that it was no one's fault except the rain-soaked road. I remember I felt no fear or anger. Some memories remain confused, all these years later. In my mind, the memory is of screeching tires, and crashing sounds, and breaking glass, but it happens after the accident, not before.

Eventually someone persuaded me to sit in an ambulance. I refused to allow them to take me to the hospital, insisting that my friends were on their way. A rather serious and concerned police officer kept her eye on me until they arrived. My memories become foggy and fuzzy after that, but I know I ended up in the emergency room later that night, and a friend took me back to my hometown the next day. My friends contacted their lawyer, who I must have spoken with, but have no memory of the conversation. I do remember crying because I couldn't write down what the insurance agent was telling me on the phone—I no longer knew how to make words appear on paper. My mother came from Pennsylvania to care for me, but I have no memory of her stay, except for a vague impression of a bouquet of red roses she gave me. My mother loved red roses.

For 17 months after that night, my life was without much sense of normalcy. The brain trauma continued to cascade from my injury for about six weeks following the accident, and the headaches lasted for years. My injury was called *diffuse axonal shearing of the brain*, resulting from my brain being shaken back and forth inside the hard shell of my skull, much like shaken baby syndrome. There was a faint crack in the bone of the skull pan behind my nose, resulting in all the sinus cavities filling with a dense congestion, some of which has never reabsorbed. When under stress or great fatigue, I find many bothersome symptoms reasserting themselves, like biting my tongue when I try to talk, or garbling my words. There's also a constant ringing in my ears, which never goes away. It's absolutely essential that I stay extremely organized in simple ways or I lose things, lose track of what I want to do or what needs to be done. Sometimes I'll find something that I forgot I had and have no clue how it got there. I know now how to care for myself, but at times, I still experience an overwhelming fatigue and need long hours or days of solitude.

After the accident, I lost my job because I couldn't return to work. I lost my health insurance because the cost of it was too much after my slim savings disappeared. My car was totaled, so the car payment I'd prayed about disappeared, replaced by an outstanding bank balance I couldn't pay. Other things disappeared too, like memory, the ability to cook, brush my teeth, walk in a straight line, talk without slurring words or biting my tongue or cheek, keep my balance, and stay awake for more than a few hours at a time. I couldn't read—or remember my daughters' names, or the names of friends.

I lost some relationships, too. People who could not understand what was happening to me chose to "blame the victim" out of their own fears that something so random could happen to them, too. They wrote off my difficulties as not being able to cope with stress or come to terms with the accident, as if those psychological phenomena did not have a real physical basis. Indeed, coping with stress *was* extremely difficult, and coming to terms with losing everything was also difficult on top of everything else, but the real issue was my broken brain, which needed time and support to heal. I was fortunate to have the support I needed, for the most part. It's truly a miracle that my brain was able to heal eventually, and I give the Creator all the credit for that.

I had great difficulty paying bills. It took me hours to get dressed. I had a hard time being around people, controlling my tears or my temper, or managing my anxieties. I had to relearn the right way to walk and talk, relearn how to cook, and play the piano, and safely drive a car. I had to relearn a sense of good judgement. I had to slowly reconstruct my life over the course of years. Eventually I recovered, for the most part, and was able to move to a new city and gain new employment with accommodating assistance, and finally have health insurance again. Without the epiphany of love that I experienced, I would not have had the inner belief in myself to push forward and try.

Ultimately though, I lost my home and was bankrupt. The insurance settlement only covered the costs of bills from banks, lawyers and doctors, and obtaining a "new" second hand car. I was also able to pay for physical therapy, finally, and buy new glasses and see a dentist. All these were things I had taken for granted before, but now each little thing was like a gift of abundance. Losing everything was a good teacher. It made me a much better therapist, and a better human being overall. Without the generous help of a network of love—my mother and family, my daughters, friends, generous people at my church who helped in so many ways, a lawyer, and Dr. Michaels, the wonderful neuro-psychiatrist who helped me immeasurably for two years (with *pro bono* services)—I would not be where I am today. I could have easily become unhomed, living on the street or in shelters, and I will always feel the sensitivity to people who survive the insecure lives created by our modern world. I'm so very grateful for my network of support.

I look at the experiences I had during that phase of my life as a type of university where I learned important lessons I always want to remember, but I also never want to have to go to that School of Hard Knocks again. The visions I've had since that event continue to inspire and motivate me to live my finest and best.

I know now that I'm loved profoundly by a benevolent universal Love, and all fear of death has departed from me. The first day I was permitted by the doctor to go for a walk around the neighborhood alone, I was so overwhelmed by the beauty of the outdoors and felt as if an endless ocean of pure love surrounded me. I stopped and stood still beside a tree, looking up at the sky through the dappled light pouring down through multi-colored leaves. It was a beautiful late-autumn afternoon in Indiana, and I realized, as if for the first time in my life, how loved and protected I really was, and that realization profoundly changed my life. I knew, at that moment, that even if I ended up living out the rest of my life in a nursing home, I would still be perfectly loveable and worthy. My value as a human being did not depend on believing, thinking, or acting in any particular way.

The unconditional universal love that filled me that day is the purest gift I have ever comprehended and encountered. It was just *there*. I didn't have to do anything or say anything to receive it—I was *in* it! I could just *be!* Sometimes I wonder why I'm still here and get discouraged and question what that near-death experience was all about, but I have the lessons of everything that has happened since then to fall back on and keep me going. I am fulfilling my purpose in life, one step, one word, one intention at a time. I have hope to pull me forward. I have been given enough light for the next step.

ℒ

Reflecting on these memories filled my mind as I drove from my office to the store on October 23, 2005. I'd not been able to go into the Sweat Lodge since the accident over two years prior, so this evening was very important to me. It was not only a sign that my brain had healed enough to handle the ceremony, but it signified a transition into a life I had felt called to during the Sun Dance Ceremony in 2003. I checked with a friend who had psychic abilities about the Sweat Lodge leader, Herb Nabigon from Canada, someone I did not know, and she assured me he was safe—"he can be trusted"—so I had no concerns about the evening ahead.

I felt calm as I parked in the store lot and got out of my car, but the wind caught the door and yanked it from my hand. Panicked, I grabbed for it, fearful that it would damage the car parked next to me. I was relieved to see that the edge of my car door had not touched the other car – there was at least enough room for a piece of paper to slide between them! The man in the other car, however, was not so reassured. He jumped from his car, screaming curses as he raced around to my side. I said, "It's okay! There's no harm done. See? There's no mark on your car!" as calmly and firmly as I could, given how startled and rattled I felt. In my job as a therapist I was used to dealing with emotionally distraught people, but that was in a relatively contained setting in the clinics where I worked. This was someone I did not know, in a dark parking lot outside of a city grocery store—the situation put me instantly on guard. When he saw that no harm had been done to his car, he switched immediately into an artificially sweet and syrupy voice, attempting to begin a conversation with me. I simply held up my hand and said, "It's okay, sir. We're done here. I need to go."

When I turned to walk toward the store the man followed me, cursing and screaming again, demanding I stop and speak with him. "What?! Do you think you're too good to talk to me? You c---!"

I was shaken by this sudden verbal violence and walked faster toward the store door. Another woman came and walked by my side, and grimaced as she said to me, "Don't worry. You'll be okay. I've got one just like him at home." As she went into the store, I realized she had likely assumed that the man yelling at me was my husband or partner. That was a sobering realization. The intimacy of violence was suddenly thrust on me in stark contrast to the ceremony I was going towards. What was going on? What force was trying to interfere with my intentions? What was this fear about?

I quickly got a bowl of fruit and headed toward the checkout counter. As I waited in line, I could see that the man who had accosted me was now pacing angrily back and forth in front of the store's big windows, looking in at me, scowling. I was growing concerned about what would happen if I left the store alone, so when I got to the checkout register, I asked the clerk if he could call store security to escort me to my car. He seemed flustered by my request and said that they had no security on staff, and that the manager had already gone home for the night. I looked outside and saw the glowering face of the man staring at me. I explained what had happened and said, "It's not safe to walk to my car alone. I need someone from this store to see that I get to my car safely."

Two very tall and athletic young men were standing in line behind me, and one spoke up, "Ma'am, if you can wait a moment, we'll walk you to your car!" Moments later, with a muscular young man on either side of me, we confidently made our way past the muttering man, who scurried to his own car and drove off. Safely inside my locked car, I waved and smiled to my escorts as I drove away.

The whole incident had taken quite some time and I was going to be late getting to John and Beth's, where the Sweat was being held on their small farm, a 50-minute drive outside of the city. Distracted, I missed a turn-off, the sign hidden in the darkened evening, and it took me a while to realize my mistake and turn around. The course correction caused more delay, so I pulled over and called John on my cell phone. No answer. Of course. They were all by the sacred fire, waiting to start the ceremony. There was nothing to do but continue on my way, hoping someone would get my message and let them know I would soon be there. I began to wonder if something was trying to keep me away from the ceremony, but I shook off those fruitless thoughts as evidence of residual fear lingering from the parking lot encounter.

I quickly parked when I arrived at the farm, took my food into the empty farmhouse, and hurried outside to walk the path to the sacred fire and Sweat Lodge grounds at the edge of a cornfield some distance away. As I drew closer, the heavy darkness obscured my path and I had to move forward slowly, following the sound of voices. There was just enough light from the faint glow of the fire in the distance for me to see trees and the outline of the large barn beside the field. Leaves crunched under my feet, twigs and small branches cracked loudly, and I heard John's voice saying, "I think that's Annie coming through the bushes."

The first words I heard Herb say to me were the ones he called out on that dark evening, "Annie, I've been waiting for you!" He told me months later that it was about 20 minutes after leaving the Sweat Lodge that night that he made the decision to ask me to marry him. Of course, that conversation took place later. It still surprises me that he knew so immediately that it was me he wanted to share his life with.

$$\mathcal{S}$$

I can see how the concept of "awesome" permeated our life together from those early moments to some of the smallest and most unremarkable of times. Herb was a robust man, of comfortable stature for someone as short as I am, with bright, twinkling eyes and warm, welcoming smiles. He embodied trustworthiness, and was so much at ease with himself that a missing arm was not seen as a handicap. I felt a solid safety in his presence. From the first conversations sitting around John and Beth's kitchen table, where I shared the story of my recovery from the accident, to the meandering conversations we had during the many trips we took together over the years, Herb and I shared many experiences and insights and found so many areas of common ground. In all our years together, we were constantly learning about each other. We would often laugh together about our simple little lives, and comment on how our most ordinary routines might seem unreal to some of the people who looked upon us as remarkable people. We certainly did not think of ourselves as anything other than ordinary folks living an ordinary life. We made our share of mistakes.

Is it possible to collect, in ten short years, a lifetime of "extraordinary awesome unremarkable?"

One of the first unremarkable moments that stands out in my memory is of that first Sweat Lodge experience together. Herb had been traveling to Fort Wayne for about 15 years to do ceremonial work before I chanced to meet him there, not by John's design, but I think by Creator's design. It was a seemingly simple coincidence that our paths crossed in that place in such a gentle manner. On the second day of Sweat Lodges, we needed cedar for the ceremony and no one had gone out to gather it.

At that time, I did not know the teachings about cedar being a woman's medicine which only women should gather for ceremony, and the women who had that teaching had not yet made their appearance for the ceremonies, so Herb suggested we go together to find some cedar.

We walked through the small stand of trees on John's property, surrounded by vigorous fields of Midwestern corn, and Herb said, "Annie, what do you think of me?" I was confused by this strange question, and a bit taken aback, so I replied abruptly, "You're a man like any other man!"

Herb persisted, "Do you think I am some kind of guru? Is that how you see me?"

At the time, I was not sure what he was seeking, but I was intensely aware of his stillness, his presence, standing there under a small cedar tree. I reached out and clipped a small sprig of cedar from the branch above my head and dropped it into the basket, and then I laughed. I got it! He was trying to find out if I was putting him on a pedestal, or if I was simply willing to let him be himself with me as a person, an unremarkable human being who happens to know some things I don't know. As I laughed, he started to laugh and made a self-deprecating joke at his own expense.

Our next conversation was Herb asking me questions about my career, how I came to be working in Fort Wayne, and what I liked about my work. Since I'm always happy to talk about my professional passions, I was off to some detailed explanations of things I had done over the years, training I had gained with no small effort and expense to myself, and explained the recent struggle I had gone through to sustain my career following the accident. He commented that it seemed to him I was a restless sort of person, always striving, and I replied, "Well, if you mean that I always want to learn more, know more, and get better at what I do then, yes, I am always seeking to push beyond where I am. I'm never content with mediocrity, and I'm convinced I'll never be good enough to simply coast. That's just who I am."

Much later, I found out that he was impressed by what I had said to him, and that he admired the knowledge I had, feeling I was much more skilled in clinical areas than he was, even though he was the one who was a professor of social work and Indigenous healing methods. I had no idea he had those feelings. When we talked about our first conversations later, I asked him, "Did you want me to tell you that I thought you were a guru?" He told me he had been relieved immensely by the words, "You're a man like any other man," because he was weary of people who wanted something from him. He wanted to share the Creator with people who wanted a connection with Creator more than anything. He wanted only to fulfill what he'd been asked to do. He heard my story about the epiphany of love I had experienced after my accident, and sharing that story connected us in the way of the heart's fire. We had a common place to meet at the heart level.

There was a relaxation in our life together, created by our ability to respect and value what the other person's abilities and strengths were. At the same time, we held a safe place for each other, had tolerance for the other person's vulnerabilities and idiosyncrasies, and had no tension, competition, or jealousy in our relationship. We protected each other's solitude. We had no need to pretend, strive, or put on any sort of act with each other. Some would say there were no games between us. I would say we had simply been fortunate to encounter each other at a time in our lives where we had finally arrived at no longer needing to impress someone else or seek their approval. We had done our own work on ourselves and were lucky to find a kindred spirit with whom we could share a life together, walking a path in a simple manner toward greater spiritual fulfillment. We were not bringing neediness to the table.

That was the kind of safety which allowed us to live together for 10 years without getting upset at dirty socks left lying around, or, as Herb often teased me, "You being the counter police again?" when I went with the dishcloth around the table before he had even finished his meal. We set limits with each other, such as the time I told him I could not tolerate a puddle in front of the toilet, or the time he let me know that Saturday morning coffee runs were his time alone, no company needed or wanted. We did not take personal affront at each other's boundaries, but respected them, stating our needs and wishes with kind or humorous words, and accepting difficulties without pouting or anger.

There were no arrogant demands or accusations between us, only requests, observations, and statements. It's extremely freeing to be able to be one's self completely, knowing that the man by your side is there because he just wants to be there, not because you are his "arm candy" or because you successfully live up to certain social expectations. There was no role-playing between us, although in some ways, we fulfilled traditional roles as provider and caregiver. The deep unconditional love and acceptance that my husband showed me consistently is a rare thing in our world today and a treasure I will always hold in my heart. It healed me of many old wounds from failed relationships.

The events in my life that first week after meeting Herb opened up a vision for my future that my wildest dreams could not have conceived. This was about Spirit. Something was happening here that was starting to clarify events that had occurred in my life over the past two years.

Just one month before I met Herb, there had been a flood in the apartment building where I lived due to a broken water pipe. Everything I owned needed to be taken out and dried, and the apartment cleaned and re-carpeted before I could move back. All that was missing was my beloved pet dog, Muffin, who had died two months prior. The first night back in my little place was disorienting. Everywhere I looked, the familiar items now returned to their place left me with a sense of detachment, derealization, and distance. I could explain it psychologically, yet I had a distinct and overwhelming vision of an empty place and saw myself moving far away from everything around me.

I whispered to myself, "I could just get up and walk out and leave it all behind, and it would be okay. I would never look back."

When I woke the next morning and prepared to go into the office, the feeling of derealization and depersonalization stayed with me. It seemed strange that a good night's sleep had not restored my inner balance. I had been displaced from my familiar apartment and then returned to a state where everything was the same yet not the same. The feelings of being caught paradoxically in a state of "being/not being" were overwhelming and left me shaken.

I arrived at the clinic and stopped by a colleague's office. "Miriam, could you come and talk with me for a few minutes? Something has happened," I said to the therapist across the hall from my office.

"Sure. What's wrong? You look upset," Miriam said to me with a concerned look on her face as she settled into the chair beside my desk. Miriam had opened her home to me and my elderly cat after the flood in my apartment, and we had gotten to know each other better over the past few weeks. I told her everything that had happened the evening before—

how I was feeling, what was upsetting me.

"I feel as if I'm not really here. Or as if I'm getting ready to go someplace far, far away and never come back. I don't know why I feel this way. I don't know why this is happening! Or what it means! I feel as if I could just walk away from everything and not look back. As if nothing matters here anymore...it's almost as if I'm completely dissociating!" I spoke with some urgency and distress as Miriam listened carefully, calmly, with the attentiveness that characterized her quiet, dignified therapeutic presence. She was a deeply spiritual person who was aware of the spiritual path I was on, and who respected different ways of knowing. She knew about displacement as an immigrant from South Africa years before and seemed sympathetic. She also knew about my struggles with dissociation in the past. She did not say much, just listened, and suggested that I simply wait and see what emerged and told me that it would be perfectly acceptable to leave work early and take a "mental health leave" if I didn't feel better later in the day. Then we both went on our way about the tasks of the day, and soon I was feeling better, grounded by the normal tasks of my job. By evening, I was not preoccupied by the previous 24 hours experience.

About a week after meeting Herb he asked me to marry him. I went to Miriam and shared, "I know now where I am going. I know now what I'm going to be doing and why I had those feelings last month of going far away. I'm moving to Ontario and getting married!" Miriam and our little circle of work friends enthusiastically rallied around me and became my best supporters and helpers over the next seven months of transitioning out of my job, out of my apartment, out of my country, and into a whole new way of life. They (and many more of my friends and family from far distances) all traveled to the wedding ceremony near Sudbury, Ontario on July 15, 2006, participating in the Sweat Lodge ceremonies before the wedding and sharing their love for me in a myriad of supportive ways. Their happiness at my happiness helped launch me into my new life. I miss Miriam—she died four years later of cancer—and while it was hard to accept this loss, she remains in my memory as a special part of my life, at a special moment in time.

My new life with Herb Nabigon was the fulfillment of a vision both of us held in our hearts. We both wanted so very much to have a partner in life with whom we could share a sane and healthy relationship, free of conflict, drama, and the effects of mental illness or alcoholism. Herb's vision was that his life could serve as an example of how one could recover from alcoholism with healing brought about through ancient *Anishnaabeg* spiritual traditions. To have a partner to share all that had been a hope and a vision of his for a long time.

Herb said one simple sentence to me that eventually persuaded me to consent to enter a marriage with him, even though we had only known each other for a week when he proposed in the centre of a bookstore. He said, when I questioned him as to why he was posing the request to marry him so soon, "Annie, I've been working on myself for 26 years to be ready for this." He said it so genuinely, with no guile, with such an open beautiful smile on his face, that my doubts about his motivations melted away.

"Well," I said, "if we're going to have a conversation like this we'd better go to my place and have some tea and talk about it there." During our conversation that evening, I asked him, "Herb, aren't there a whole lot of wonderful *Anishnaabe-kwe* lined up in Ontario just waiting for you to ask this question?" I was teasing him, of course, but I was also half serious, knowing how the real world works and realizing that significant boundaries were being crossed, unknown borders being breached. I knew that, realistically speaking, we were going to face more resistance than just doubtful family members if we entered into a marriage.

Herb replied, seriously without any smiles, "Well, yes, you are right, but you see, I had to wait to be the right person for the right person." He didn't say he was the right man for me, or that we were soulmates, or that he had been waiting for someone like me for 26 years. He said he had been working on himself to be ready for this. He saw what I had to offer, and it was right for him. He recognized me and my gifts and what it was I wanted for my life. He put out his hand and simply asked me to share my life with his and he gave himself completely to share his life with me.

I thought it was very amusing that he admitted other women wanted to marry him, but I also liked that thought quite a bit. It confirmed for me that he was putting some rational thought into this special connection we were feeling, and also that he was not going to pout or be emotionally devastated if I refused his offer. He was not needy, or trying to manipulate me emotionally, or get me to take care of him, or find a way to take me to bed—there was ample opportunity for all that in his life if he so chose. He wanted us to build a life together, to share a real life with me. I had been looking for real for so long!

But I had a few more questions, and then a few more, and finally I said, "Herb, what are you going to say to those people in your circle who will be upset with you for marrying a white woman?" I was concerned how we might handle that, being well aware that we might face pushback. In fact, we did. I lost a few friends over this issue, and faced disdain from some new people, but I chose to let that go. It is their problem, not mine. I know who I am—I will continue to live out, in my own way, my commitment to Spirit, to justice and reconciliation, to love.

Herb's immediate and strong response to my question was to say emphatically, "I'll tell them to go f--- themselves!"

We both laughed, each imagining the shock of those words and then I insisted we would make some agreements before I said yes. We talked long into the night about what was important in our vision of a marriage relationship. We got the structural stuff down right at the start. It was more like negotiating a business agreement than a romantic fusion. That was new, and it felt very good to me.

We did go to bed together that night, not to share sex, but to gently hold each other and sleep, and when we woke in the morning, we saw each other with tender awe and love and respect, both amazed we were now joining our life with a person we barely knew. We were embarking on what could only be considered the greatest adventure of our lives so far. I took him back to his lodgings with our friends, Debbie and Mark, who were to take him to the airport, so our time together was brief.

The beginning of our courtship came after the commitment to marry and was conducted mostly over the phone in long hours of conversation between Ontario and Indiana while we got to know each other and work out the issues that couples have to address in the early stages of a relationship. We were not young anymore and saw no reason to wait to marry, so his sister and I began to plan for a July wedding in Ontario. It was a big step of trust, but a bigger step for our family and friends.

Our friend John, who had introduced us, sat me down one evening and interrogated me as to my motivations. I knew our friends and family were looking out for us. I tried to explain that we loved each other, and felt we were being called to a higher level of spiritual life by joining our lives together and that it was okay to trust the love that was at work here. We knew what we were doing, and everything was going to be okay. Friends, like family, had to take it all on faith, and we knew many people were wondering if we were in our right minds. Herb's brother-in-law laughed and said, "I'll believe it when I see it!" when Herb's sister, Dorothy, informed him of the wedding plans. We had a wonderful, gentle, and thorough courtship, and it seemed as if we had known each other for a very long time when we finally moved in together in June 2006.

I didn't see Herb again until Christmas, when I visited his children and family in Ontario, and then again in February, when he spent a week with me in Fort Wayne and met my daughters in Goshen, Indiana. They were hesitant to open their hearts to this stranger, but, as adults, were willing to tolerate their unconventional mother's decision, although they did voice their concerns strongly to me later. At Easter, I made another short trip to Ontario, and then, over the Memorial Day holiday in 2006, we met again in International Falls, Minnesota, after my brother Marty, who lived there with his wife, Diane, and their children, told me in no uncertain terms that if the family was going to admit a new person into the circle, we needed to all have time to sit together and talk. My mother, then, also had the opportunity that weekend to meet Herb and his sister, Dorothy, and a family friend, Peggy Adams.

Some months after Herb's death, Marty wrote me a letter reminiscing about that weekend.

> *I don't remember the exact dates, but I believe it was a little over 10 years ago, Herb and Annie and Dorothy and Peggy Adams came to visit us at our home near International Falls, Minnesota. [May 2006]. I think everyone that weekend was trying to figure out what this business was of learning to relate to someone new, someone whose life story, clan, and culture were different from the others. Herb was gracious, willing to teach, willing to listen, and willing to share. It was obvious*

that such willingness was just his way of living.
In my family of origin there is, among various personal idiosyncrasies, some history of uncured mental illness. Among my earliest memories of toddlerhood is the memory of an old woman dressed in grey, rocking in a chair, away upstairs in the 3rd-floor bedroom of our old duplex. Two long flights of stairs up from the kitchen and dining room lived my "crazy grandma," next to the attic. She was my father's mother and had suffered much personal loss in her life. My mother and father apparently felt duty-bound to rescue her from the County Home for the indigent and bring her to live with us.

The arrangement was decidedly unhealthy. My father was struggling between jobs. My mother was about 47 years old, had two children in elementary school and a small toddler who was the "surprise" baby just before menopause. In all honesty, from what I know of my family of origin, my mother and father simply did not have the personal resources of mind or soul to adequately care for the crying, muttering, rocking, feces-smearing old woman whom they took into their home. There was anguish, there was shouting, there was hitting; and there was the facing of the stark reality that no matter how duty-driven my mother felt to provide care for her mother-in-law, that mother-in-law needed to go back to the County Home. So, she did, and there she died.

For some reason the rocking chair stayed on in the house. When I bought the house, the chair came with it. And because I'm ever the optimist hoping to fix broken things, I took that antique chair with me through 4 moves, always thinking that someday I would strip its old paint, re-glue its wobbling joints, restore its beauty, and redeem its haunting history.
We were gathered under a small canopy amongst the towering pine trees behind our house. The old green and chipped-white rocking chair became one of the seats we had there among the trees. As Annie and I shared with Herb & Dorothy this story of our Grandma, and the chair, and the unhealed wound in

*our clan of Grandma's mental illness and our mother's abuse
of her, Herb extended grace to us and offered to pray for the
healing we needed. A fire was lighted in my little fire bowl
there, sage was burned for the appropriate smudging, prayers
were brought to our Creator, we were touched, the chair was
touched, and tears were shed. We were thankful for that
small ceremony to bring closure to a painful piece of our past,
represented in the old green and chipped white rocking chair.
That night some unexpected rain came and blew into the area
under the canopy. In the morning the seat of the old rocking
chair was puddled with water—**red water**.*

*The next time I moved, the chair was sold as an antique project
at the yard sale. Without its story. Its story had been prayed
and washed away, its symbolization of pain was resolved, and
it was just an old chair. Miigwech, Herb, my brother.*

ৡ

Herb's ability to bring healing to the broken hearts and minds of people
was filled with love and grace and simple belief in the Creator's power.
He generously shared his abilities with my family from the start and
was deeply loved by all of us. He always said of his abilities to heal, "It
is not me. It is the Creator." His vision that he could help people by
sharing the story of his recovery from alcoholism through the traditions
and teachings of his culture was a driving force in his life and all his
relationships.

His book told the story of his own healing. Not many Indigenous
people of his generation were published authors, and Herb worked on
his book for 20 years before he found a publisher through the help of
his good friend, Dr. Georges Sioui. Many friends, his first wife, Sheila,
and our friend, Heather Campbell, helped him shape the book. It's a
remarkable story, not only of his healing from addiction, but also of the
traditional teachings which restored his identity and gave him a way out
of the destructive effects of addiction and away from the cruel forces of
genocide and colonization. Story telling has always been a traditional
way of transmitting knowledge in Indigenous cultures, and the style of

storytelling weaves in and out, backward and forward, to share wisdom based in nature and spirit. I always loved listening to Herb tell stories and I still love re-reading his book, always gaining fresh insights.

During the months leading up to our wedding, he was deeply involved in the final editing process with his publisher, McGill-Queens University Press. One of the poems he had wanted to include could not be incorporated into the publication because it was impossible to obtain the author's consent, so he asked me if I would write a poem to replace that one, which is how my poem, "Spirit Road," came to be included in his book. After our wedding, we gave a copy of the book to my mother. As she read it, she said to us, "Annie, how on Earth did your poem end up in a book about Indian things?" Herb had a good laugh about that one.

Herb's vision of helping just one person find a clean and sober life meant, to him, that his own life would have meaning. *The Hollow Tree* came out in 2006, the year we were married, and when he received his first author's copies, he was overcome with emotion. This was a major turning point in his life. There were no tears, just a mild agitation as he paced around the apartment, and then he said, "Annie, I'm going downtown to find someone on the street to give a book to."

That seemed a bit extreme to me, and I made a joke about it. "Are you giving it for free, or charging a dollar or—what?" Then he told me about his idea that he should just hand out copies of his book and hope that someone would be helped by it. I think, looking back, he just needed a bridge to thinking of himself as a published author, a successful academic, and not the "street drunk" he had once seen himself as. It was a huge shift for him. The mental and emotional stretch was light-years apart. Herb always felt somewhat ambivalent about identity and belonging, and this was reflected by his occasional struggle to see himself as a successful university professor and a well-known traditional Elder. He would sometimes say, "Annie, I'm just a bush Indian."

We often talked about that in oblique ways, seldom directly or analytically, and usually in the form of a story or sharing a memory. Sometimes that stretch showed up in unexpected places. Once, while walking along a sidewalk in Toronto, Herb stopped and turned to me, pointing to the corner ahead of us. "Annie," he said, "that's where I used to stand and sell pencils to get enough scratch to buy another bottle of whiskey. And over there," he pointed to a new building, "there used to be a little park where I would sleep sometimes." We stopped and stood there silently for a few minutes, and then he turned to me and said, "Once, I brought my son, Clem, here and showed him this corner and told him about sleeping in that park and selling pencils. Clem got tears in his eyes."

Herb was very moved by those memories and went on to talk about the friend who found him there one day and helped him get a bed in a shelter. His friend brought him a new set of clothes the next day and told him about a program Herb could get into if he wanted. There was no judgement, just acceptance and a quiet offer of help. The day after, Herb took his friend up on his offer. It was one of the countless times people gave a helping hand to him when he was trapped in his addiction.

We would occasionally stay at a small boutique hotel in Toronto on Madison Street, close to a tiny jewel of a park, tucked discreetly beside the Madison Manor. It had one path curving gently in from the sidewalk to a cluster of wooden benches surrounded by shrubs and tall grasses, flower beds and rose bushes interspersing the random foliage and patches of grass. It only took a few minutes to follow the curve of the path back onto the sidewalk and on toward the busy street lined with stately University of Toronto buildings. For the brief five or ten minutes we would spend in the park, we had a reprieve from the busy city, a gentle return to nature in the heart of concrete and bricks. It was a place I came to think of as "our" little park, and each time we went to Toronto, I looked forward to stopping there.

As we headed out that evening from the hotel toward a favorite restaurant, passing by the park, I said, "Let's stop for a bit and rest on the bench there," but I no sooner said that when I saw the benches were occupied by a diverse handful of people of varied ages, casually lounging, laughing, passing their bottle around, occasionally giving a shout about something, and I said, "Oh, no, the riff-raff are there. Let's not stop."

Herb stopped. He stood firmly in front of me and looked at me with an unusual expression I had not seen on his face before. He said, "Annie!" sharply. I immediately knew what had happened. I felt ashamed. I had embarrassed myself. "Annie, look! In there is the next Native Human Services professor. In there is the next graduate with a master's degree. Don't think of them as riff-raff because that was me once, long ago!"

This was one of the most important lessons Herb ever gave me. In just a few words the reality of a whole world shifted, and it brought me face to face with my distance from my sister, my brother, my neighbor, my love. It brought me face-to-face with my ever-present white privilege. This lesson is an integral part of my vision. I have to carry my responsibilities with humility and courage to do the transformative work calling me. No apologies can erase responsibilities, and it is my intention to carry accountability wisely as I move forward in this life.

"I am *so* sorry," I said. "Please forgive me. That was wrong of me, and I'll never allow myself to do that again." And I haven't. The lesson was important. It was not something I had never intellectually encountered before—it was something I needed to learn with the heart, not just the mind, not just in an academic sense, but in a real-life sense, and it is a lesson that I need to keep learning for the rest of my life. I do not get to empty my "backpack of privilege" and throw the backpack away, no matter how tired of it I am, or how outdated its contents. It's my backpack, it's my responsibility to work every day to carry forward the messages of healing from division and woundedness. The greatest gift of help I have received for this task came from my husband, Herb. The gifts of our life together give me strength to continue my journey.

There are no more "riff-raff" in my view of the world. I am there. Since that time, I make a point of giving some money to the person who asks for it whenever I have an opportunity to reach out. I stop and look at people and ask them how they are and if there is anything that I could do for them. That acknowledgement is important to me. It's my way of calling myself to accountability—to response-ability. Just walking by and not looking at the human being on the street is not acceptable. The greatest gift I can receive is the gift of someone accepting the help I am able to offer. I have received so much help in my life, and the only way I can repay it is to "pay it forward." It's none of my business, really, what they want, or why. I have no right to judge, only an obligation to respond. I learn in that way what the Universe wants me to know at that time. I really know so very little.

When Herb and I walked a street together in Edinburgh, Scotland, during a visit there many years ago, we passed by an area where a lot of people hung out, milling around, looking for something, looking for nothing, just needing a place where tourists, shoppers, and business people hurried by, oblivious to the suffering in sight. We stopped. We talked to some people sitting on the cold sidewalk. We gave what we could. I remember that day clearly. We were *together*, seeing people who were just like us. We are all in this together.

Herb suffered from alcoholism. The illness of alcoholism, like other addictions, is one of the cruelest diseases a human being can suffer. It robs a person of the brainpower they need to overcome the progression of the illness. Brains can become "hooked" on the surges of dopamine triggered by a process or substance, which activates certain areas of the brain. Brains can even become addicted to feeling miserable! The ubiquitous presence of alcohol as a social beverage makes it extremely difficult to eliminate from one's life if the vulnerability to addiction is present. Sometimes thoughtless people do not even consider making non-alcoholic beverages available in social situations, which makes it even more challenging for those who choose not to drink alcohol for whatever reasons.

Alcohol always deceives in one way or another. There's a time and a place for social drinking, but for some, one drink is one too many. This is to be respected. Humans are vulnerable to the lies of alcohol, even if they are not addicted. I think one of the roles of people with alcoholism, like Herb, who had such a passion for helping others with the same affliction, is to help shine a light on the issues around it. Those who suffer, trapped in the misery that comes with alcoholism, need the help and support of caring, consistent, non-judgmental, knowledgeable people. Family members and friends lose too, and their suffering can be great, lasting a lifetime or many generations. Few affected by this cruel illness will have an opportunity to recover.

When Herb lost his right arm in the drunken encounter with the train as a very young man, he lost other things as well. It was no longer easy for him to navigate out in the natural world, as he had been able to do before. His strength was different, and his sense of balance was off. The characteristics that made living in the bush manageable, and which had allowed him to succeed with only a few brief years of formal schooling, were no longer possible. Along with the loss of his arm there was a brain injury that went unidentified, but which he knew without a doubt. He had lost the "photographic memory" that had so enabled his life up until that time.

The accident occurred near his grandparents' home in White River at the railroad station. His grandfather still worked for the railroad and lived in a company house right by the tracks. Herb left a party there, which had been held in his honour after returning home from a trip to the United States. He was heavily inebriated and decided to try and catch the train to Sudbury on an impulse. One small slip as he reached to grab the boxcar, and his arm was under the wheels. This slip changed the course of his life, setting him on a whole new trajectory of life without his right arm, onto a path that would eventually lead him out of the natural world and into a professional one, culminating in an academic position at Laurentian University. The path out of alcoholism was long and difficult. Herb was one of the lucky ones who recovered, but he always said he could never afford to drink again. He was able to travel, in the last ten years of his life, to many countries to talk about the spiritual traditions that saved his life and nurtured his vision of what a full, vibrant, healthy life could be. His vision was that others would be touched by his story.

His relationships with the people whose lives he touched while on those travels were significant in his life, and his death impacted people from Ireland, Scotland, Mexico, Brazil, Argentina, the United States, New Zealand, and all over Canada. His relationships with people were immediate, fully present, and not limited by time. You could know Herb for only a brief moment, and he would feel as close to you as someone he had known for decades. His unique, timeless manner of relating to people never failed to amaze me. He was always "adopting" people.

ક

Herb was not a perfect person, nor did he have a perfect recovery from his own alcoholism. The scars remained with him all of his life. He had suffered deep psychological wounds from the treatment received from clergy and teachers at both the residential school in Spanish, Ontario, which he attended briefly, and the small day school at Pic Mobert Reserve. This type of educational system existed around the world, run by dominant church-state institutions designed to oppress people, control them, and change them. Crimes were acted out on children in the most horrifying and unforgiveable of ways. It was genocide (a process continuing to this day), and is recognized by the United Nations as a crime against humanity.

Herb had been hungry in the residential school, had been beaten for speaking his own language, and had his long braids cut off, not done gently either. He carried memories of the footsteps of the priests at night in the dark dormitory room, and the sobs of the little boys who were brought back later in the night. He was always afraid they would take him too, but said in later years that because he was from a big family and had relatives at the school, he was somewhat protected. The children most preyed upon were the most isolated ones.

The torture children were subjected to in residential schools and boarding schools across North America, Ireland, Australia, and on other continents, has created a cascade of historical trauma that has yet to be adequately addressed or fully comprehended. In Canada and the US, it was not only Catholic Church institutions that were the culprits. Governments enlisted every religious organization available—*including the Mennonite Church*—to carry out its effort to "kill the Indian in the child." Like all other Indigenous peoples, Herb spent much of his adult life recovering from the effects these policies and actions had on him, his family, and his people. The damage is not just in the past, but is intergenerational. In his university role as a professor of Native Human Services, he worked toward solutions and ways to empower people, to heal from these historical wounds, but he firmly believed it was the traditional teachings of his people that held the healing for him.

Many people have the perspective of only one form of knowledge, based in the style of education from North America or Europe. If we're fortunate and literate, we may learn about older styles of European education by reading about them in history or social studies books. There were "hedge schools" in Ireland, and the Bardic training of the Scots, ways of knowing that were systematically taken apart and suppressed by British dominance. The oral training of the *Griots* in certain African cultures is still alive at places today. Other Indigenous peoples around the world have preserved their unique forms of knowledge transmission in certain areas. The varieties of Indigenous ways of knowledge training around the world are typically discounted and suppressed by the dominant, mainstream ways of knowing.

Few people alive today have experienced the benefits of one of these older forms of education. Herb Nabigon was one of these people who benefitted as an adult from five years of intensive traditional training from his Elders. He was mostly untouched by modern education until his entry into residential school at around the age of eight years old. He was only there a few months. He had landed in the harshness of Spanish, Ontario with a rudimentary understanding of English and writing (thanks to his parents' efforts at home schooling) and was able to print a hidden message to his father in the first letter home. The class had been told to copy what the teacher put on the blackboard—"I like my school. My teacher is nice. We have good food," etc., etc. *ad nauseum*. In between the lines Herb printed in tiny letters, "Come get me."

Unlike many of the children who were subjected to the harsh residential school system, Herb had a father, only a few years out of the Canadian army after WWII, who was not inclined to abandon his first-born, this child he had not seen until Herb was almost four years old. His father took a train from Pic Mobert Reserve southeast to Spanish, Ontario, near the north shore of Lake Huron, and walked to the residential school where he demanded that the priest return his son to him.

All Herb knew was that one day his father showed up and took him home on the long train ride, and then the whole family went into the bush near Lake Tripoli, several hours by train ride east of the town of White River. He remembered his grandmother making him hide under a bed in the little cabin when she heard the train stop on the tracks that ran close by the hidden camp. Herb's father had arranged for the engineer to stop and leave a copy of the *Globe and Mail* newspaper, and collect whatever gift was left in exchange, but his grandmother was frightened that the Royal Canadian Mounted Police (RCMP) would come looking for the children. Nine of her sixteen children had already died in various residential schools long before Herb was born.

The *Globe and Mail* was instrumental in Herb's home education in that little one-room cabin deep in the northern Ontario bush. He studied at the rough kitchen table by the wood stove, where his mother taught him arithmetic, and his father assigned him passages in the paper to read. He had to struggle to figure out the words, and he was also required to write a paragraph or two about the article he'd read. His father would sit and talk with him at the end of the day about what he had written, and if there was a discrepancy, Herb had to go back, re-read his assignment and write again. He partially attributed his ability to write papers much later in his academic career to his father's disciplined use of the *Globe and Mail* while they lived in the bush at Lake Tripoli.

The freedom and safety Herb had in his childhood years in the bush shaped his core values, along with the chores he was assigned, and the structure of the natural rhythms of life in the bush, which was not an easy life. Survival required hard work. There was no running water, no electricity, no indoor toilets or plumbing, no television, microwave, washer or dryer, no video games, movies, or roads for bicycles, no telephone, or corner store to buy junk food. There was just the leveling power of living a subsistence lifestyle: chopping wood, carrying water, washing clothes and scrubbing floors, learning in nature, playing with people and pets, swimming in the lake, encountering the animals of the forest, and being part of a close-knit community.

Herb's memories of that time were vivid. He could describe the life he lived in the bush with various extended families, occupied with the endeavors of fur trade and basic survival. It was a time of happy memories for him, a time when he learned the knowledge of animals and fish, birds and plants, in his mother tongue, *Anishnaabemowin*. He learned the prayers of the Catholic faith, but also remembered his grandfather giving tobacco offerings in the bush as he said his prayers privately.

Herb did not attend formal school again until he went to day school for a few years at Pic Mobert Reserve around the age of 12 or 13. That was a very confusing and perplexing time for him, and perhaps did more damage than the months in the residential school, impacting his psychological development in ways not fully comprehended until the last ten years of his life. In that day school, he was exploited by an emotionally manipulative and cruel female teacher, a young immigrant from post-war Europe who briefly taught school in the small, isolated Reserve near White River, Ontario. The betrayal and abandonment by this teacher left deep scars that contributed to many difficulties with relationships as he went through life, and he never fully recovered from the consequences of that experience. There was no compensation for that damage, which went unrecognized for so long. He had never talked about those realities, or fully comprehended their impact on him until a few years after we were married.

When Herb was around fourteen years old, his father enrolled him in Scholard Hall in North Bay, Ontario—a boarding school with a good reputation—and it was there where Herb flourished for the first time in a formal education setting. He enjoyed his brief time there, and it opened up a window onto a wider world for him, but he was unable to finish the first year of high school following his mother's death in the spring of that school year. The grieving young teenager who made the long train ride home alone from North Bay to Pic Mobert First Nation lost the opportunity to have the good education his father hoped he would have.

Herb never returned to school, and by the age of fifteen and sixteen was going into the bush again with his father to pursue the life of a hunter and trapper. That, too, was not to be, because Herb had no love of that lifestyle, or talent for it. He hated the feeling of cold snow falling from a tree down his neck and checking the traplines in the water on frosty winter days. He had little success in setting the traps or shooting when hunting for food. While he and his father were walking the trapline together one day and Herb wasn't finding many animals in his traps, his father said, "You won't make much of a hunter and trapper, my boy. You'd better find a job."

After that, he did find work in other places. He worked on the construction of the Trans Canada Highway between Wawa and Thunder Bay, cut line in the bush, washed dishes at the logging camp in Manitouwadge, and had a few jobs with the railroad companies after his cousin taught him Morse Code. The railroad work lasted up until he was fired for getting intoxicated, sleeping on the job, and giving out free passes to his relatives, but he enjoyed the work a lot and used to tell funny stories about his time with the two different railroad companies. His dream job though, was to drive big trucks. He never expounded on the attraction to the power of driving those trucks, and never realized that dream. It became part of the nebulous, misty past. It was not until

Herb was in his twenties, after losing his arm, that he returned to school to improve his education. His father sent him to Toronto to get him out of Pic Mobert. As Chief, his father used his insight to move his son out into a wider world. He had the wisdom to recognize Herb's intellect and knew that, if Herb could grasp the opportunities, he could build a better life for himself and not die on railroad tracks on an isolated Reserve. Herb never graduated from elementary school or high school, or even university before he entered Carleton University in the Master of Social Work program. He was able to adequately thrive, and sometimes excel, in academic settings, usually with help from friends or his first wife, Sheila. He was gravely addicted to alcohol by that time, resulting in the eventual collapse of his marriage and separation from his children. By the time he graduated from Carleton in 1977, he was ready to enter the modern world of professional work, but first he took some time off to go drinking.

On a train to Toronto, after a party to celebrate his graduation, he forgot the bag that contained his diploma and papers. He never again had a copy of his graduate degree, but he also never saw a need to replace it, saying that the university could confirm his degree for anyone who needed to know—and what he knew, he knew. He didn't need a piece of paper to prove it. Among the papers left behind, however, was the only copy of his thesis, which he co-authored with a classmate.

Thirty years later in 2007, while I was working on my Doctoral degree at Laurentian University, I found a reference to Herb's Master's thesis for Carlton University's School of Social Work. I was able to get a copy from the University of Manitoba on interlibrary loan, made a copy, and had it bound. Herb could hardly believe his eyes when I presented it to him as a gift. He shared many stories with me of the trials and challenges he faced as he struggled to complete his thesis, a study on the adaptations Indigenous students made when leaving their homes on Northern Ontario Reserves for high school in the city. He treasured the relationships he formed with the students deeply. Teaching was one of his passions. It was a substantial thesis, one that his advisor had encouraged him to publish, but he never bothered. He was still too occupied with his addiction to attend to much else. Only later in his career as an academic did he become interested in publishing, and he managed to amass a long list of publications by the time he retired in 2012.

The healing traditions of his culture gave Herb a way to deal with the pain in his psyche once he was free of alcohol. Recovery does not come smoothly, or overnight, but emerges through daily accomplishment over the course of years. I heard him say once that the person in recovery with the longest stretch of sobriety is the person in the room who has gotten out of bed the earliest that morning. Herb needed to be careful at times how close he allowed himself to come to other people who were not healed from their addictions, or to people with serious mental health problems.

In the context of the ceremonies, Herb had the tools to deal with these issues, but it was important for him to limit his personal relationships at times, or even to cut them off altogether, in order to maintain his equilibrium. His sobriety was his priority. Staying busy in positive pursuits and pastimes was a major coping strategy in his life and helped him to be happy and make his contributions to life. Music, movies, traveling, and visiting friends and family all helped him create a life worth living, but the primary activity that helped him was doing his work in Ceremony.

When he was growing up, Herb had been negatively impacted by the effects of alcohol on his family and community. There were residual fears and betrayal traumas left from those experiences. Losses in romantic relationships, a failed marriage, failures in other interpersonal relationships and employment situations, all converged to create specific areas in his life where he had a barrier, an internal screen that stopped him from fully grasping the context of some situations. This contributed to missteps, mistakes, and betrayals, leaving some people with feelings of hurt, disappointment, abandonment, and anger of their own. He was able to repair some of those relationships, but others he could not, extending the wounds of ignorance and hatred into future generations. Traditional Elders are not magically perfect people. They have to deal with their own "rascals," as Herb once wrote. Herb was a multifaceted man who generally did a pretty good job of maintaining balance, respecting his "rascals," and being responsible. He couldn't control how other people perceived his efforts, but he was always aware of the need to work on himself.

All of these issues were similar to mine. I could identify and share with Herb some of the losses and failures in my own life. While I hadn't been subjected to the types of abuse he experienced in residential school, I had experienced other types of abuse and had deep difficulties while growing up. I also survived two rather dysfunctional marriages, from which I never fully recovered until attending the Sweat Lodges and praying for healing. Prior to meeting Herb, I had spent years in counseling and Al-Anon, which helped me to understand how to see myself with honesty and take personal responsibility for my own healing journey.

My own failures in relationships, mistakes, betrayals, and pure stupidity haunted me, but in the ten years leading up to meeting Herb, I had experienced much healing through a lot of hard work and, in my opinion, miracles. Thanks to our efforts, we were able to come together in our marriage without either of us dragging along a ton of old baggage and unfinished business. We had the basic tools to make things healthy and beautiful between us.

ॐ

The additional factor complicating things for Herb is what complicates life for Indigenous peoples all over the world: the lasting scars of colonial oppression and outright genocide, the ongoing oppression and theft of land and resources, and the tremendous internal distances each Indigenous person contains within them in striving to adapt, accommodate, and sometimes assimilate. Herb's intellectual powers and network of relationships gave him a step up in being able to grasp some of the things needed to adapt and master the skills to live in a modern world.

For me, as an individual from the mainstream world (although I, too, still struggle with my own "invisible minority" identity from origins in a rural Mennonite sub-culture), it was a real challenge to be able to immerse myself in a world of relationships with people who had suffered direct effects of genocidal forces in their lives. When I married Herb and moved to Ontario, I did not integrate into a typical Canadian culture. I moved to *Anishnaabeg* territory and had a tri-cultural challenge in

Enough Light for the Next Step | 53

adapting as an immigrant. I was intensely aware that I lived on treaty territory and had responsibilities to learn to share appropriately.

Herb was Oji-Cree, which explained the differences between his dialect and the language from Manitoulin Island, close to Sudbury, Ontario, where we lived. I faced many challenges in trying to learn his language in the early years of our marriage. Understanding things when people from different locations were speaking in "the language" remained difficult for me. I didn't get too far in learning to speak *Anishnaabemowin*—it's one of the hardest languages in the world to learn—but my favorite way to learn words and phrases was by singing with the women's drum circle I was invited to participate in while we lived in Sudbury.

One evening, after my first language class, I learned some new words in an unusual way. That evening, Barb, the traditional coordinator at Shkagamik-Kwe Health Centre, had been teaching a small group of us how to properly introduce ourselves. It was fun to go around the room saying the new words to each other, laughing together at our mistakes, and finally getting it right. After the lesson was over, I said to Barb, "May I use the phone to call Herb and ask him to pick me up?"

She smiled and said, "Of course," and then added, "When he answers the phone just tell him, '*Ambee, Kwazee!*'" I repeated the phrase several times as she struggled not to laugh at me.

"What does it mean?" I asked.

"Oh, he'll know what you mean," she replied, smiling. "It's just telling him to come get you."

When Herb answered the call, I repeated the phrase, "*Ambee, Kwazee!*" with the exact same inflection Barb had modeled.

His laughter lasted for several minutes before he finally managed to choke out, "Annie! What have you been drinking?!"

Puzzled, I replied, "What?"

"Never mind, I'll be right there." He was still laughing as he hung up the phone. By then everyone in the room was roaring with laughter, and my puzzled question to Barb went unanswered.

While Barb giggled away, one of the other women said to me, "You just told your husband, 'Come here, old man!'" Then I started to laugh, too. It wasn't in my vocabulary to call my husband my "old man." He delighted in telling his relatives what I had said, to their great amusement.

⚘

I also learned stories from his family of their genealogy and discovered that a distant ancestor was from Scotland, as were my own Campbell ancestors from my maternal grandfather's side of the family. A few years before Herb died, we were able to travel together to Scotland and see the places where our ancestors had lived, exploring distant ancestral roots. We started out for Oban one afternoon, planning a ferry trip the next morning to the Isle of Iona to visit the monastery site there. Following poor advice from someone I knew, I had not reserved a room ahead of time, and we could not find a place to sleep in Oban that night.

We took the road out of Oban, south toward Glasgow, hoping that along the way we would find something soon. I saw a little sign by the road pointing off into the meadows and hills that read, "Sheep Fank Cottage B & B," so we turned and followed a winding country road that narrowed until the hedges on either side brushed the car, and the pavement turned into a dirt lane.

I began to feel frightened as we wound through the unfamiliar fields. There was no place to turn around, and no way of telling what lay ahead. Herb was tired and grew more silent as we drove, seemingly into another time and place, where fairies and ghosts might rise to follow us. Dusk was beginning to fall, and I was losing my sense of direction when the hedges ended, the dirt path turned into pavement, and pleasant houses with neat lawns lined the way. We were relieved to see the sign "Sheep Fank Cottage" ahead of us on the lawn of a beautiful, modern house. After some negotiation, we settled into a comfortable room, and though there was still some light outside, Herb was soon snoring.

I walked down the stairs, through the lounge, and out to a bench under a small ash tree. A stream rippled nearby, and flowers scented the evening air. The cottage sat on a hill and spread out before me was a scene of fields folded around distant hills dotted with sheep. Birds circled above, their calls ringing through the clear evening air. In the nearest field, a flock of Canada geese were settling in for the night. Our host pointed out some distant ruins, and told me about the rock palisades not too far away. He and his wife had moved there recently after they retired from teaching near London. Ice climbing was his favorite sport, and they had been coming up from London for decades to winter hike and climb the palisades. Scotland was home now—they were happy there and pleased with the income the B & B generated for them.

I wondered about his experience as an English person living in Scotland, but I didn't inquire, not being sure of the politics of the situation and not wanting either to be a cause of insult or to demonstrate my ignorance. I knew from friends of ours that in many areas of the country, the English were barely tolerated by the Scots, if not outright disliked, much the same as when we were in Ireland a few years prior. I wondered if our host felt like an alien in his new home.

My own experience as an American coming to *Anishnaabeg* territory resonated with what I imagined he, too, might face. I was much more sensitized to the First Nation situation in Canada than the typical immigrant, but I seldom found a setting to explore my feelings and thoughts about my experience. Sitting in that cottage garden in Scotland, viewing ancient ruins in a distant pasture, I wondered if this man of some small privilege ever gave a thought to the politics of his personal choices, where it placed him, and how he had worked out his relationships there. I wonder now what I might have learned if I had asked about the personal and the political in that little garden. What lessons might we both have learned about how to live in the borderlands?

Living in intimate contact with Herb, his family, and his community opened my eyes to what it really means to immerse one's life in the world of survivors of genocide, oppression, and deep trauma. Because we were both trained as social workers and shared a spiritual vision for our life together, we had a common language of sorts, but mostly we just lived together and loved each other and learned, every day, how to create a life worth living. We didn't do a lot of intellectual talking about these matters, which were always present with us, one way or another, acknowledged or not. I was fortunate to be able to share life with someone who accepted me just as I accepted him, someone who did not try to change me. We loved each other unconditionally, and the "shadows" and "rascals" of politics usually remained at bay.

Herb and I had the benefit of being able to rely on the teachings of the Medicine Wheel, the Seven Sacred Teachings (or Grandfather Teachings), and the spiritual traditions that he was taught by the Elders who had helped to save his life. He taught me as much as he could of what he knew, and we used these teachings to solve our problems, to guide our way forward, to give us what we needed in order to live a good life together.

The teachings of the East Door (which he gained through his training with the Elders) held special meaning when it came to Vision. It was what we tried to keep before us in setting a foundation for our life together. His own words from an unpublished transcription explain eloquently the foundational story of our life together. It begins with the story of "The Little Boy," which Herb always shared whenever doing a Sweat Lodge ceremony, and concludes with the Seven Grandfather Teachings:

In a place before time, on our Mother the Earth, the Creator was walking in the woods and he heard a little boy crying. He asked the little boy what was wrong and the little boy responded to the Creator by saying he was afraid of his parents because they were fighting most of the time. All of the other children in the community were also afraid, and all the children ran away from the community. This information from the children really disturbed the Creator, and he was wondering what to do about this situation. After much thought about the children, he decided to gather all the children and he took them into his home. While the children were in his home, he taught the little boy about the Four Directions and the Seven Grandfather Teachings. He began by teaching the little boy about the East Door.

The east is where the sun rises. The sun is about renewal. The beginning of a new day. If you look towards the east in the morning you will notice that the sky is red. If you look deeper at the plants in the springtime you will also notice that the roots of the plants are red. The blood of animals and people is also red. There are also only four blood types amongst people of the world. As you can notice, red is a very important color. All of life is renewed in the spring. For example, the moose, and all of the other animals, plants, birds, fish, and insects have their young in the spring. The spring is a time of new beginnings. All of life requires a special time saying that is so. You will notice, after a good meal, you feel better. There is a strong relationship between food and feelings. If you eat good food you feel better, likewise, if you eat a lot of junk food you feel bad. This teaching of good food reminds us how important it is for us to stay healthy. A healthy person can see a long way on. There is a strong relationship between good food and feelings and vision. The East door of the medicine wheel teaches about vision, renewal, feelings, and animals. The Fast in this direction is about seeking a vision, it helps us to see a long way. In a traditional fast, we abstain from food and water. Food is represented in the east and water is represented in the west. The East Door and the West Door are the busiest doors. The east is where babies are born every second of the day and the West door is where we exit from, when we join the spirit world. There is traffic in the East all of the time and there is traffic in the West all of the time. Because there is so much traffic in the East and West, these doors never rest.

So, the little boy understood the teaching of the East and the Creator also said to the little boy that the turtle sits in the East, the turtle spirit, and he assigned the turtle to heal the broken hearts and broken feelings of the people, to mend those broken hearts. So, when we pray in the East, we ask the turtle spirit to mend the broken hearts and broken feelings of ourselves and our community.

As you know the sun travels from East to West, and at midday the sun is facing south. The colour in the South is yellow. Mankind has always understood the sun to be a timepiece. So, the South informs us of time and the colour yellow. As you know, they say the sun heals everything on the Earth, including our minds, through the optic nerves. The gift in the South is time and relationship, and the colour yellow symbolizes the people of the world from Asia.

When the sun travels from south to west, in the evenings the sun sinks below the horizon and everything turns black and we know from our experience that when we see black clouds in the sky, we know that it will more than likely rain, so dark clouds bring us water. Water cleans the air, cleans our bodies and nourishes all of life.

As the North wind comes in late November, this part of the world is covered under a white blanket and we know from our experience that the cold North wind and the snow reminds us to seek shelter to keep from freezing so the North wind is teaching us to care for our survival. The grandfather that sits in the North is the bear.

Finally, at the centre of the Medicine Wheel, green represents Mother Earth. This direction also represents the fire in our hearts. When we pray in the lodge, we pray for the fire in the sky world, the Creator's fire, our fire in our hearts, and the fire at the centre of the Earth. They align themselves and provide perfect balance, the Anishnaabe way of understanding how to heal the Earth. Those are the four directions.

As the little boy was descending from the Creator's home, he looked from the other side of the moon and when he viewed the Earth from the other side of the moon, he saw a sweat lodge. The sweat lodge had a cedar trail so he was very curious to discover what the lodge was so he descended to the Earth and he looked inside. To his amazement he saw seven grandfathers sitting inside the lodge. He hesitated to go in and the first grandfather said to him, 'Come on in, biindigan,' and the little boy said, 'I am too small, they will not listen to me.' The first grandfather said to him, 'That is okay; we will

help you teach the people. We will teach the people wisdom.'
Wisdom is a teaching that helps us understand how things
repeat themselves in life and patterns. When you understand
patterns, and wisdom, and how night follows day and day
follows night, you can gain wisdom by seeking to understand
that.

The second grandfather says, 'We will teach the people love.'
Love is the absence of fear; there is no Rascal. Rascals are
defined as inferiority, as envy, resentment, not caring, and
jealousy. That is how we define fear and evil, and love has no
Rascal, no evil.

The third grandfather says, 'We will teach the people bravery.'
Bravery means that you face your foe with integrity and you
move forward in a good way to face your enemy.

The fourth grandfather says, 'We will teach the people
respect.' 'Re' meaning again and 'spect' meaning 'to look.'
Respect means to look again at everything. Look twice at your
decisions, look twice at the people, at your family, look twice at
your community. The reason you look twice is to see the good
and the bad in everything you encounter in life.

The fifth grandfather says, 'We will teach the people
humility.' Humility just means there is only one small part
of creation—you. Just like there is only one 'Herb' in the
world and I understand that. What humility does is it
counteracts arrogance. Arrogance is not good for our spiritual
understanding.

The sixth grandfather says, 'We will teach the people honesty.
Honesty is what you see out there and you interpret it, and
you give your interpretation to what people say or don't say.
Honesty is how you maintain and develop your integrity so
we will teach the people to be honest with each other.'

Finally, the seventh grandfather said, 'We will teach the people to speak the truth.' There is only one truth—your truth. As there is only one 'Herb,' I will use myself as an example. I can only speak my truth, not anyone else's truth. The grandfathers teach the people to speak their truth whenever they relate to each other or as we relate to the spirit world. We will speak our truth when we go into our lodges. Sometimes people ask: what is the difference between honesty and truth? Honesty is a value of integrity that people understand the world over, and every culture values honesty. Likewise, everybody values and honors truth, but the difference is there is only one truth, your truth, the truth that you speak.

'This is what we will teach the people—the seven grandfathers,' Creator says to the little boy. 'If our people understand these teachings of wisdom, love, bravery, respect, humility, honesty, and truth, that will counteract the violence and it will help the people move forward in a good way. We will teach them how to live and to live well.'

When Herb shared these teachings, it was always basically the same story, with slight variations, but with the emphasis on the vision of mending broken hearts. Herb and I never said or did anything to break each other's hearts—we had had enough of those experiences in other relationships. We never indulged in the kind of anger that couples sometimes allow themselves to fall into, where harsh and cruel things are said and accusations made, or where silence reigns and smooths the feelings between them.

When we had differences of opinion, we voiced them honestly, and we let each other know where our boundaries were, but we did not try to control each other. We took time to be patient, to be kind, to be rational, to express ourselves honestly and fairly, and to focus on the vision that was part of the teaching of the East Door. We sought understanding above all else. We took our prayers seriously, asked the Creator to help us, invited the Turtle Spirit to come to us and heal our hurts, and we sincerely tried to follow, with kindness and respect, where we felt the Creator indicated we were meant to go, supporting each other and not interfering with the other person's path.

The kindness we practiced together was as simple as the small coffees Herb would bring me from Tim Horton's, or the tea I would fix for him and carry to the couch where he was watching the evening news. It was as intense as the times I woke from a nightmare and he comforted me. Eventually, he said, "We'll deal with those nightmares. We'll go to the water and you find a stone and bring it home." So, we did. When we got home he prayed over it, had me hold it and talk to it, and then he said, "Put the stone by your bedside when you go to sleep. Let it absorb all those things you have nightmares about and the stone will take it away." Since that time, a bad nightmare is a very rare thing in my life, unlike what I experienced before.

THE SOUTH DOOR

TIME AND RELATIONSHIP

When we received our wedding pictures after our ceremony in July 2006, one of the photos looked as if it had been taken through a yellow filter. A closer look at the background revealed the figure of a large, very old Indigenous face, filling the entire backdrop behind us. It was faintly outlined and appeared to be looking at us as we stood together at the reception table. It was a rather unbelievable photo and we puzzled for a long time over how this figure had appeared in one of our wedding pictures.

I thought perhaps it was a distortion of the lighting, or some mistake in the development process, but Herb pointed out aspects of the figure that could hardly have been staged, or an artificial construct, or a distortion—the downward cast of the eyes slightly varying from left to right, the clear outline of brown hair falling over shoulders, the distinct outline of facial bone structure in a light brownish-yellow tinge. Herb told me he believed it was the figure of one of the three ancient Spirits who had been watching over him for a very long time.

Herb was an adult when he became aware of the three Spirits, but he never spoke of it to me until we were with a Medicine Man who was working with Herb. The Medicine Man commented on being able to see the three Spirits. "Two of them are male, but one is a female," he said. Herb had no difficulty with this understanding. It was not a matter of believing "in" them—it was a simple acceptance of a reality and a truth outside of the normal range of human physical perception. He believed that these three Spirits had saved his life when he lost his arm and had protected him during the years after his mother's death until he found sobriety.

Herb had no difficulty with the concept of Spirit being compatible with natural science. For him, Indigenous science simply spoke to a realm of reality that was currently unmeasurable by statistics or present-time scientific methods. Indigenous science was part of the Natural Law that he'd grown up understanding and absorbing through his life in the natural world of the bush—air, fire, and Earth, the rivers and lakes, and the animals with whom people had relationships. Indigenous knowledge had Spirit of its own and that Spirit of Knowledge could be recognized when one spoke honestly about one's own truth. Herb respected the Spirit of Knowledge and recognized it as an integral part of living the good life— *Minobimadiziwin*. The spirits who watched over him were part of this wisdom.

⍥

Our first six years together were busy years as he carried a full teaching load at Laurentian University while I worked hard to finish my doctoral studies. I had the opportunity to do some teaching at the same university and enjoyed that very much. During those years, Herb also traveled to Mexico several times, to New Zealand, Argentina, and Brazil as he accepted invitations to speak at academic conferences or other international Indigenous conferences. There was a book launch, book signings, workshops, and, in addition to all this, the traditional work that he continued to do whenever asked. Herb was always very busy, but he also knew how to relax, and we had the opportunity to take vacations and visit family who lived far away.

We visited Ireland together with a group of other people interested in restoring the Indigenous spirit in relationships with the land and with the people. There is a YouTube video of Herb giving a talk on the stone medicines at the standing stone in Berra, Cork. Those times were important in strengthening our relationship, and we had so much enjoyment in being able to share that trip together, as well as the trip to Scotland, where he was able to spend time with the people of Gal Gael, in Glasgow, and share his teaching and a Pipe Ceremony. On that same trip, our friend, Alastair MacIntosh, arranged for him to be interviewed for a Sunday morning program on the BBC. He spoke about his experiences and healing from the ravages of cultural trauma, residential school, and alcoholism. It meant so much to him to be able to share his teachings with a wider audience, and he genuinely loved being able to talk with people who wanted to learn.

ℒ

When we moved to Pic River, I was looking forward to the experience of living near the bush, and maybe developing some skills for harvesting food. I knew I was a pretty good shot from past experiences, but I didn't own a gun, so hunting moose was out. A relative did teach me how to set snares, and I also participated in berry picking excursions. I was content to enjoy the moose meat that other people harvested "for the Elder" and I was helpful in as many ways as I knew how. Once, Herb told me he thought I would have been a "good bush wife," but his descriptions of the extremely hard work his grandparents and parents did made me doubt that. Life in the bush is a good life, but it's a very hard life, and there isn't much time to sit and read books.

Living in a city almost guarantees that one will not encounter moose in any predictable way. A moose might occasionally wander into town, but that's usually rare enough to generate news coverage on at least the local level if not the national level, depending on what else is going on around town. I rarely saw moose when I lived in Sudbury, except occasionally when driving north.

Living north of Lake Superior on a small First Nation Reserve was a different experience for me, and most certainly *does* guarantee encounters with moose. They'll be at the bush line along the roads during certain times of the year or crossing the road, or even standing directly in the road looking at you (don't beep the horn!). I never saw any in my front yard or walking down the street, although one of my near neighbors did have one standing in her yard early one morning.

Herb had promised to take me moose hunting when I moved to Canada, but after my arrival, I learned that he'd never actually hunted a moose for himself. He had helped as a guide on moose hunts with "tourist hunters" from the United States as a teenager and had a story about that, but it was always unclear to me if he was partly joking with me in telling his story. It was yet another one of the "stories" he told me as a test to see if I could discern the teasing from the facts. We had quite a lot of fun with his embellishments over the years and he loved nothing more than when I had an "ah ha!" moment and caught him at the game. I learned that, in presenting himself as "moose hunter," something much subtler was being communicated to me, and I developed the ability to hear his metaphor, listening to the implied meaning. He was telling me something about capability, and the feelings he had about capabilities he lacked. This is an Indigenous way of telling a "truth story."

When he finally did go moose hunting, it was a crisp, autumn day in 2013. He was 71 years old, going along on a moose hunt for the first time in a very long while. He and his *niitaawis*, Duncan, left in the early morning darkness to drive the hour and a half to the site Duncan had chosen. They parked the truck and walked to where Duncan was sure the moose would be. They sat and waited, and Duncan made the calls a mating moose would recognize. Herb, wearing a bright orange hat, took a handful of tobacco from a pouch in his brown and tan camouflage rain jacket, and said a traditional prayer in his language, facing all the four sacred directions and greeting Creator, asking respectfully for the gift of meat so that the people could live.

Almost half an hour after calling the moose, and sitting still and waiting, the breath of an animal could be seen at the tree line as it cautiously emerged from cover. Duncan carefully lined up his target and dropped the moose with an instant kill shot to the heart. He is a very good hunter, but the moose was far away and it was an ordeal to get it back to the trailer behind the truck. Having a four-wheeler made it possible for these two old men to wrestle approximately a thousand pounds of moose back to the truck site after field dressing it and cutting it into quarters. In field dressing the harvested animal, they removed and discarded the entrails and whatever was not going to be used, and saved the heart, nose and tongue, which are considered delicacies. The other parts were left in the bush for scavenger animals and birds to share the feast. It's the natural way, and their ancestors have been sharing the life force of the moose in this fashion for thousands of years.

The rest of the day was spent further butchering the carcass down by the mouth of the Pic River, where it flows into Lake Superior. The whole family participated, including Duncan's young grandchildren. River water washed the blood from the trailer and from the hands of the ones handling the meat. Herb was happy, and kept laughing and saying, "I put down the tobacco and Dunkie put down the moose." When skinned, the portions of the moose were hung in a neighbor's walk-in cooler for a few days, and then I helped with the cutting of the meat, wrapping and labeling it. We worked together—my sister-in-law Dorothy, Duncan, their daughter, Carol, and Duncan's brother, Robbie––with Herb bringing the coffee and talking as we worked outside in the cool air and bright sun at trestle tables set up in front of the garage beside Duncan's house.

I felt so close to the real world, the natural world of that day. The sky was a crisp, beautiful blue with the trees on the mountain behind the Reserve dark against its brightness. Gulls, crows, and ravens circled overhead, hoping for scraps. I wondered if the spirits were there with Herb, and I thought about what it was like to have that protection around us all. The memory of participating in that traditional activity is one I will always treasure.

Herb had such joy in him that day and spoke of so many pleasant memories of times in his childhood, memories that seemed to bubble up with the laughter and joking we all shared. It made him happy that I so calmly and willingly participated in the hard work of getting meat ready for the family, and it felt satisfying to stack our share in our freezer at home, ready for winter meals. The event went a long way to healing something in us, bringing something together, bridging a distance not of our creation, but one that shadowed us all the time. The separation came from the great gulf between the different cultures in which we grew up. Our love and respect for each other was a strong bridge across a divide not of our making. The divide did not interfere with our life together.

Herb said, "We get our strength from the meat. The moose gives the sacrifice of its life so that we can live. It is a sacred thing." We were strong, too, and our strength grew in the final years as we grew closer together. A bond like that is not broken by a simple separation of physical death. Looking back now, it's a memory that has become a metaphor for the sacredness of our relationship, and I like to believe that the Spirit that showed up at our wedding was there that day, too, watching over us.

When I drove from our home out the long road to the TransCanada Highway and into town to my office for work on cold winter mornings, I watched to see if by chance a moose might be nearby. They're seldom out in the mornings, but people talk about seeing them at night. If the clouds do not block the sun, one can see a snowy, foggy mist rising from the bush with the sun shining through. The beauty of these winter mornings is always awe-inspiring for me. The memory of his life stays with me here, moves me still, often to tears, when I see this winter morning splendor. I look for the breath of the moose as he did that day of hunting for food, but I never see what he saw. The memories of his stories feed my heart just the same.

Herb would often say, "Our lives are like the breath of the moose on the cold, morning air." We are here on this Earth for just a short time, like a puff of breath, with nothing to show of our presence when we die. In his case, though, I think the breath he left in his words will travel far into the future as the teachings he shared are re-shared, over and over again, in many places around the world. Many of his students carry his teachings forward into coming generations, and his friends and family continue to live out the teachings absorbed over the years of learning with him.

Breath of the moose—I will always search to see it, however far and long I go into the future. The time I spent with Herb is like the breath of the moose. The ten years we shared went by so fast that I was left feeling breathless frequently in the months after he died. It felt as if I had to learn to breathe again, to lift the weight of sorrow and loss from my heart so new breath could fill me. Grief became a journey where I lived in Herb's world, alone and unsure, needing to completely re-order my life to move forward. It took me a long time to feel that things might get better, not just different, and I'm grateful for the ways in which I was helped by many different people.

ॐ

Ten years and two months prior to Herb's death, he sat me down for a serious talk. We were in Toronto, visiting and doing some shopping before I returned to Indiana after my first visit with his family. Herb said to me, "You don't have to do this, you know. I might not live for very long."

"What are you talking about, Herb?" I was puzzled by his statement.

"Well, I have diabetes, and my health might not be so good ten years from now," he said quietly, looking at me.

"A lot of people live a long life with diabetes. My father was eighty years old when he died and he had diabetes," I replied, a bit stubbornly.

Herb continued to look at me for a while, and then he softly said, "Annie, the Elders told me when I would be going. I only have about ten years left. I'll understand if you don't want to marry me anymore."

We sat together in silence for a while and then I hugged him and simply said, "Then that's ten years we'll have together that we wouldn't have otherwise. I'm not changing my mind."

It was the only time we talked about that, but when he suddenly became very ill in January 2016, I remembered the conversation in January 2006, and I understood the power of knowledge, of words, of beliefs, and I was in awe that I was seeing spiritual realities unfold in front of me. Until that point, I don't think I fully comprehended the inner reality Herb was grounded in. He let go of his physical life so gently and calmly and went to the other side peacefully. Many of the old Elders know about these things, and I was honoured to see this reality unfolding in front of me, as unreal as it felt at the time.

I'm gradually growing into my own understanding of these realities in my life as I move forward alone. Remembering and pondering upon the lessons I received from my partnership with Herb helps me reorient my life following his departure, despite the struggles I grapple with. I occasionally feel depleted and discouraged, but I only feel that way because I sometimes feel lost, without my moorings, as if I'm a tiny boat on the waves of a huge ocean and have no anchor, no harbour in sight. I sometimes feel frightened and angry about seeing the known structure of things around me beginning to crumble and disintegrate. I do not always feel a sense of equanimity about life being "like the breath of the moose."

I live now with the feeling that life is more transient, fragile, and mysterious than I have ever understood. Stepping back from my immediate surroundings allows me to observe and say to myself, "I see

I am living my life. I see that I am like the breath of a moose." Whatever I am feeling and experiencing, I also see myself going through that experience. When I can be wise enough to embrace what is happening at any given moment, it is easier to allow what is happening to just happen even if I hate what is happening. There is little I can change outside of myself. I still struggle in life like any other human being, but I am more able to be compassionate toward myself in that struggle and to recognize it as part of something larger than me. I see trouble and problems as a small part of a much bigger picture, and I invest effort towards keeping my view balanced with acceptance. I can see all the ways by which I give myself loving care being balanced by the ways I am unable to be self-compassionate. I strive to extend that compassion to the larger social world, and the troubled planet as a whole.

Herb used to say that people were being so destructive to the Earth that She would take matters into Her own powers. He said the Elders had told him this time would come, and that many innocent people would die. The changes were inevitable and necessary, but many innocent people would suffer. He said it was minutes until midnight.

I'm glad he's not here to live through this anymore. I wish life could be simple and safe, and that willfully ignorant, greedy, power-hungry despots couldn't sit in the seats of power. I know humans have the ability to see this and move against that clock, turn back that clock from almost midnight, and turn back the destruction, but I don't know if humans have the will and resolve to do the necessary hard work. I wish everyone could know and embrace the good life—the *minobimaadiziwin*—of which Herb spoke so often.

There were times we sat by ourselves in the living room of our house north of Lake Superior and looked at each other, talking about how glad we were that we had this gentle, simple, quiet life together, away from the chaos and "rascals" of the rushing world, one that so often seemed lost and confused and bent on self-destruction. We had our little refuge together there, and while it seems far away now, I only have to go there in my memory and feel the comfort our life together gave us.

Early in the mornings, Herb might be taking a shower, or fixing his coffee, or listening to the news on the TV. Often, he would light some sage to smudge, or shake his buffalo hide rattle with the eagle claw to acknowledge Spirit. He would let our dog, Maccabee, out on the front porch, and his barking would wake me. If it was the smell of coffee that woke me, I'd get up and drink a cup with Herb. He always made me coffee but could never remember if I took sugar with it or just cream, so he would always ask me. I liked that. I liked to hear him say, "What do you want in your coffee, lovey?"

Herb liked to hear me play the piano, but I usually played when he wasn't around because my piano playing skills were pretty rusty. He liked classical music and often listened to it, but country music was his favorite. He especially liked Waylon Jennings, and Jesse Coulter, and the "old" country singers. He had stories about drinking with George Jones, and reminiscences about encounters with other well-known celebrities over the years. He told me about his memories of hearing his mother sing along with the old battery-operated radio in their cabin by Lake Tripoli when he was a little boy. "She could sing those old country songs pretty well," he said. He liked them because it brought back memories of his mother, and those early days of his life, which seemed so much happier to him, before residential school, before she got sick, before she died.

Herb felt very close to his mother, who was so young when he was born while his father was away in the army during WWII. He was close to his maternal grandmother, too, who had delivered him under a big old pine tree outside the little cabin on the Pic Mobert Reserve. One time, he took me to the spot and said he wished the tree was still there. He never knew what had happened to that tree. It was on that spot that his grandmother gave him the name "*Maahng-ese*" (Little Loon). She told his mother that he would not understand the meaning of his name until he was in his forties, a prescient statement since it was after the age of 39 when he started the journey toward living a sober life with the traditions of his people.

After Herb died, I learned that his father had not actually fought overseas, and I pondered for many months on what could be the meaning of his embellishing the story. I imagined that a little boy growing up without a father might have some questions, and perhaps people around him explained that his father had gone away to be a soldier, which meant to fight in the war. Herb was so proud of his father's shooting abilities, and in his later years, constructed the story of his father being a sharpshooter in Italy. The real story is not quite so romantic. His father came home from a position on a New York hockey team, enlisted in the Canadian army, and completed training. The unit he was scheduled to be shipped out with, heading for Italy, was delayed by several weeks. They never left their location in Quebec because one of the men purposely shot himself in the foot to avoid being sent into battle. The whole unit was held up as a result, and by the time they were ready for deployment again, there was no longer a need for their services.

Herb's father came "home from the war" like so many of the other men from Pic Mobert, and Pic River and the north shore area, seen as heroes by the people at home. Not long after Clem Nabigon, Sr., was discharged and returned to the Reserve in Pic Mobert, he was elected to be chief of the little community, a position he continued to hold for a long time. It was only much later after he remarried that he moved the family to Pic River First Nation.

One of the memories I heard Herb share many times arose from an event where he observed his father setting a powerful boundary with some government officials. The government of Canada in those days was engaged with the government of South Africa, consulting on how to refine the Apartheid system there based on the Canadian system of Reserves. Visitors from South Africa came to Pic Mobert First Nation one day accompanied by the Indian Agent and an RCMP officer, as Herb recounted it. When Clem discovered that they were there to learn how to create and run a Reserve, he decided it was time for them to leave. He rounded up some other veterans with their long-guns, and Herb watched them order the government officials to leave. It made a big impact on a little boy to see his father act in such a powerful manner.

Another story he told about his father involved a visiting RCMP officer and a challenge put to him to shoot a partridge sitting in the bush some ways off. The RCMP officer apparently did not believe Clem's assertion that he could shoot that partridge from where they were standing and challenged him to demonstrate. When Clem shot the partridge in the head, the amazed officer asked him, "Where did you learn to shoot like that?" Clem's reply was, "I trained as a sharpshooter in the army." Perhaps these memories conflated with other things in Herb's aging mind as a belief that his father had been a sharpshooter in Italy.

What is illustrative for me are the things not said more than the stories recounted, however embellished. What he did *not* talk about were the ambivalent feelings for his father which were present in his life, stemming from the early absence, and the later violence that he witnessed after his father started drinking heavily. These ambiguous losses left their mark on him emotionally.

One of Herb's early memories was of a drinking episode at his childhood home, which deteriorated into a fight between his parents. When he shared that memory with me, he said how scared he was that his parents might kill each other, or kill him and his little brother and sister, with the guns they were waving around and pointing at each other. He was so terrified and had not seen that type of thing happen before. He believed he was around ten years old when it happened, and as an old man, he told me, "I can still feel that fear whenever I remember it."

♨

There were many other memories that were more pleasant, and nothing made Herb happier than sitting with friends and relatives, laughing and recounting the stories of the past fun times. Some of the memories came from the camp at Lake Tripoli, and when the chance to visit there arose, he willingly cancelled plans to attend a conference in Cuba to go camping at his old childhood home in the bush. This was quite an adventure, because Herb's idea of camping at that time in his life was to settle into a comfortable room at the Holiday Inn.

In 2008, we climbed on a train leaving the White River station and travelled into the bush, headed for Lake Tripoli and the area Herb remembered as a child. With us were his niece's young daughter, his sister, Dorothy, and her husband, Duncan, whose father had been in Scotland, where Duncan was born, during the war. The train we were on stopped in what seemed to be the middle of "nowhere northern Ontario" and we unloaded our tents, canoe, camping gear, rifle, and food from the baggage car. We stood and watched the train grow smaller in the distance, leaving us with the penetrating quiet and beauty of the surrounding forest.

The first morning in our tent, under the tall spruce and pine trees, we woke to the sounds of bird songs echoing through the forest. The early morning air was still cool although it was mid-summer, and Herb struggled to get out from under the blankets and rise from the air mattress on the ground. I woke more completely when I realized the rustling and cursing was my poor husband trying to get out of the tent for a call of nature. "I'm trapped!" he grumbled. "This wasn't such a good idea!"

"Sweetheart, just pretend you're in a Sweat Lodge!" I giggled, as I rose to help him get some leverage to stand. I heard him laughing as he walked off to the rudimentary waste pit Duncan had dug the day before.

For four days we lived in the bush. I canoed, bathed in the icy lake water, cooked over the open fire, and hiked with the others through the thick forest with only the barest glimpse of a track. Eventually, we found the site of the old trapping camp. The log cabins which once stood there had long ago melted back into the forest floor, and we found only a few dirty glass bottles, a half-buried metal bed frame, a big rusted washtub, and the outline of a foundation. The big rock Dorothy remembered climbing up and sliding down as a little girl was now shrunken to just a little rock, maybe waist high. She got a lot of teasing over that rock shrinking. The big birch tree she remembered was gone, and not even a hint of an outhouse could be seen.

It's a long stretch from the late 1940s and 1950s into the 21st century. In that time span, Herb and his family travelled from the life of hunting, trapping, picking berries, and living in the safe nest of the close family groups, which lived, laughed, worked, argued, and loved together, into a modern world. What was normal then was foreign now and so very missed, and what might have been was also grieved. Some tears were shed in the forest that day, and new roots grown in our relationship with each other.

The first time Herb drove me to his home Reserve at Pic River First Nation (now known as *Biigtigong Nishnaabeg*), we followed the TransCanada Highway from Sudbury to Sault Ste. Marie. When we started up the north shore of Lake Superior toward Wawa, Herb said, "I have a tap root that goes down deep beneath this territory, so deep I feel like I'm home whenever I see these trees, this water. This is my place. I always come back to home here."

After we crossed the Pic River, deep and sluggish with chocolate-colored water, and turned back through the bush toward Pukaskwa National Park and the Reserve, I had a growing sense that I, too, could feel at home here among the trees, near the great lake—*G'Chi Goomig*. The spruce and tamarack, the birch and poplar and Jack pine, and especially the sacred cedar trees—all were reminiscent of the forests I had lived among as a child in the mountains of Arkansas. The cedars were slightly different, and the rocks were not shaped like the "pancake" rocks I remembered from childhood, but the feeling was similar. Something in our hearts connected in this territory, something without time and space delineating distance, something that drew us into its mystery, building relationships and collapsing time.

Not long after we moved into our new home at Pic River First Nation, we were sitting in the living room, still a bit awed that we actually had such a beautiful, peaceful place to live, and we talked about the long and different journeys we had each taken to get there. The conversation drifted to Herb's memories as a young child, and I asked him, "What is it like to realize that, in your one lifetime, you stretched from a life in a small log cabin on the Tripoli trapline and at the Pic Mobert Reserve to being a retired university professor and author, living in a fully modern home with all the technological comforts of the 21st century?"

Herb began to reminisce about his early life and talked about how much of his time was spent out of doors, in the bush, and how much he missed that. He got a very distant and emotional look on his face as he said how special it was at that time in his life. "It was a different language …and it's something about the imagination…it's a feeling, out there in the bush. I can't explain it." He got tears in his eyes and grew silent. I wanted so much to understand more, but my imagination could take me only so far. I could only draw on my experiences as a little Mennonite child in nature in Arkansas, which was a very different life. We came from such diverse worlds, and while our lives had intersected in profound and powerful ways, we were both keenly and tenderly aware of our different origins, yet it was not divisive. We were curious about each other's experiences and open to learning. That never changed in over ten years together. There was always something new to learn in our relationship.

Herb drew strength from the teachings that he held and he felt very powerfully connected to the spiritual realities carried by those teachings. It anchored him. He was someone who knew how to live in the "eternal now," but he also understood the importance of teachings about time. He said he preferred to be "early" to events because he said his grandparents and parents had taught him that "the right time" was important and showing up and being ready when people were ready was part of respecting the connection between time and relationships.

I sometimes was confused about his orientation to time when he forgot to show up for something he had agreed to do or got there late. He would say that "when the time is right" was the only time there is, and also, that there was no such thing as "native time," but that in the true traditional way, one would always be present in a place or with someone "when the time was right." While his grandfather may have told him that "real Indians" showed up early, not late, Herb was a man who could be so absorbed in his present moment that he would forget he was expected to be at a class, or give a lecture, or conduct a sweat. Quite a few people could tell you stories about Herb not being where he had agreed to be.

I think it is just these types of experiences that perfectly illustrate what he strove to teach about time and relationship. He could illustrate by his own life the importance of attending to one's relationship with others, and to one's commitments. The "contrary" stance of forgetting, of not attending to relationship, highlighted exactly how important it was. In learning from Herb, the Elder, living in a traditional way, I came to see that teachings are not only given in a presentation, or a written form, or a lecture, or a teaching story. They are given by living a whole life, one not perfectly consistent, yet one that can illustrate what to do by showing what not to do.

Time issues did not seem to worry Herb too much. He accepted what was, and if he was "late" or others were "late," he didn't usually find it to be too much of a concern. Other times, he would insist on being "on time" or getting there early. I learned to just roll with it and let Herb be Herb, and his relationship with time wasn't really my concern. My concern was being in right relationship with my husband.

I did learn through all of this a new understanding of my own relationship with time. Having always been chronically challenged to get places on time and finding that stressful, I was able, in the ten years I lived with Herb, to grow into having an easier ability to show up at events in a timely fashion. I truly grasped the importance in my relationships of having a good relationship with time itself, being more fully present in my environment, and being able to "stay in the flow" of things rather than pushing against something. It has been liberating, and I enjoy each moment more as I am able to be more fully present with both myself and others. I learned how to not worry about being on time and just simply be there "at the right time."

The teachings of the South Door of the Medicine Wheel that Herb spoke of were about many things, but most of the time he spoke about his understanding of time and relationship. He talked about the sun in the sky at mid-day facing into the south direction. In the Cree teachings he gave, he believed this direction was symbolized by the colour yellow, and that this was the "Door" where people of the Asian nations were represented. He believed that, as we understood the position of the sun and the movement it made around the four cardinal directions of the Medicine Wheel, we could learn about the right relationship between time and relationships, and by reflecting on these teachings, we could centre ourselves better in a right relationship with ourselves, each other, all of creation, and the Creator.

South Door teachings help me to reflect on what it means to know the difference between the gift of a relationship and the commodification of a relationship. When time and relationships become commodities, the whole world suffers and each individual soul suffers, as does every aspect of creation. When time is a commodity, and relationships are commodities, then it's easy for power to be distorted and for people to be enslaved physically, socially, mentally, and in every imaginable way. We would prefer the illusion that slavery does not exist in today's world, but that is not true. The reality is that almost everyone is in some form a "wage slave," and many millions of people are victimized by human trafficking across the world. Sexual slavery and exploitation misuse the gift of relationship. There seems to be no end to the combinations and permutations of how humans are able to distort the gift of time and relationship and degrade themselves and everything in their environment in the process. We can be helped by reflecting on the teachings on the South Door of the Medicine Wheel. Humans can change and heal through the gift of time and relationships.

Herb taught that when the gift of time and relationship is respected, there is balance, and we can live in freedom from exploitation. With the teachings, we gain control over ourselves. There is no control over others. Without a good understanding of relationship, and the dedication of our time to focus on the gifts of relationship, our souls starve. Starving souls are suffering souls, and humans with starving souls are living only in survival mode, where the focus narrows down to a limited spectrum of gain/loss, live/die, or "me vs. you." This leads to brutal competition and exploitation, and everything then becomes a commodity, which further destroys the gift of life.

Because of the teachings of the South Door, which I received from my husband, I've been able to understand that the Creator's intention is to give love generously to *all* of Creation, myself included. The sweet abundance of the life around us is open to me and to everyone who my life touches. There is a beauty in living in love and experiencing every relationship, in every time, as a gift. When I can see that the suffering souls that have touched my life have been part of the Gift of Life to me as well, I am humbled and awed. I give myself the time to see, listen, reflect, and respond.

I'm not preoccupied with myself and my own survival concerns when I achieve this balance. That understanding is so liberating, and my intention is to live that out as much as possible, yet I'm a human biological entity on this planet, embedded in my environment with my own unique experiences. I will not achieve perfection in my ability to live out the teachings of the South Door and the Medicine Wheel. Perfection is not what it's all about. What I do is put thought, energy, love, honesty, and intention toward being able to grow in my understanding of time and relationship. I know that, at each step of my way, all the guidance I need is gifted to me, all the forgiveness I need can flow from my own heart into my own mistakes, and in the right time, I can be reconciled to myself and all of Creation around me. When I first moved into Herb's apartment in Sudbury, his sister, Dorothy (my "denguay"/sister-in-law), was helping me put up some pictures I had brought with me. I was having difficulty centering a small "scherenscnhnitte" (paper cutting) which my mother had made for me. Herb told me to just forget about it. I got upset and began to argue with him and he looked puzzled. Dorothy stepped in and laughingly said, "Annie, this is denguay training now—do what you want to do!" Herb and I looked at each other and both of us started to laugh. I finished what I was doing and he stepped away. We both accommodated each other in a spirit of knowing we weren't going to be perfect and errors would naturally occur. I think neither of us were entirely happy with Dorothy's "denguay training" in that moment, but it worked to help us both just accept each other and remind ourselves of what really mattered—our connection.

This, for me, is a great freedom, a great gift, something I aspire to live out, and I am eternally grateful to Herb for introducing me to these concepts and supporting me in developing my own insights about the teachings. There was a synergy between us as I worked with him, learned with him, and lived with him. We loved our life together and lived it fully, recognizing it as a gift to us from the Creator and honoring our time and relationship. The simple life we had continues on in my own life in new forms as I continue to reflect on these things and share the gifts I've been given.

About ten years before I met Herb, I experienced a series of deep, wrenchingly painful experiences in my life, initiating me into new ways of living, thinking, and being. During that time in my life, I had a "vision dream," and the sensory impact of the dream has stayed with me ever since. I can easily recall it to my mind, which I think is odd considering how many memories I lost after my accident. Part of the vision dream was experiencing three wolves racing in the snow beside me as I walked in a winter forest. I felt the snow thrown up by their legs as it blew against me. I saw the colours of each hair in their pelts moving as they raced. I heard the sounds of the snow and their breath as they flew past me. I met an Elder from the Menominee Nation during that time and offered him tobacco, asking if I could share my vision dream with him and receive his thoughts about that. He listened to me carefully and deeply as I sat and talked with him, then was silent for a while before saying to me only one sentence, "You have been given many gifts, and you will help many people."

When I look back over my life and ponder on my most difficult experiences, the times when I experienced great vulnerability or woundedness were often times when I was very strong. It seems paradoxical to realize this now, but it's a simple truth. Our greatest strengths can emerge where we may be weak, and our greatest weaknesses may become our strength. These years after losing Herb are teaching me much about strength and weakness.

Growing up in my Mennonite family I felt that I had to be competent, self-sufficient, and strong all the time in order to be worthy, loved, and valued. That was my family's "rule," and to show weakness in any way was to fail. We were to be perfect "...even as your Father in Heaven is perfect." It was our job to take care of others, to give to everyone around us and never ask for anything for ourselves. We were God's hands and feet on this Earth, which is true to a certain extent, but for us to need other people, or to fail in any way, was shameful. Needing help of any sort meant being unworthy, and that was to be avoided at all costs. Not surprisingly, this burden of shame exacted its own terrible cost and left me ill-prepared to head out into the world with a grasp on genuine strength and self-confidence. It's what I had learnt—not necessarily what had been intended for me to learn.

I remember an event when I was around 19 years old. My father was disabled from cardiac problems and my mother became distraught and angry. The ministers from their church came to the house and delivered a gift of money. The church had "taken up an offering" to give to my parents who were experiencing financial challenges. This act of kindness and generosity did not comfort and humble my mother—she felt humiliated and shamed.

I remember exclaiming, "Mom! We give money to people all the time! What is so wrong about accepting a gift given in love?" She would not adjust her beliefs and suffered for years remembering that event. It feels sad, now, to look back and consider the messages I received as a child, the terrible conflict I was placed into with such an unbalanced belief about generosity. It was always for others, never for oneself. Any deviation meant an accusation of selfishness would follow, and to be selfish was a great sin. This environment didn't do much to teach me anything real about either selfishness or selflessness. It did not help me to value myself. It left me profoundly mystified.

Developing self-confidence requires an ability to experience failure without shame, to grow and adapt successfully to challenges without always having to be "right." Coming from a shame-based culture, I relied too much on being everyone's friend, became a people-pleaser, and had few tools to deal effectively with strong emotions such as anger, fear, desire, and joy. Anger was frightening. Resistance was futile. Being quiet and self-sufficient and never needing anyone was the high standard I held myself to but always failed at miserably.

This way of life brought me no joy, which I ended up looking for in all the wrong ways. I'm a strong-natured individual, outspoken and opinionated. I'm not natured to be quiet and passive. As a child, I was loud, impulsive, over-active, and bold. It was not in me to be part of "the quiet in the land," which Mennonites traditionally aspired to be. Perhaps too much of the Campbell genetics carried through to me, but this is what I received, which was, in a way, a gift, helping me to survive. Developing a calm, self-confident, assured assertiveness was something I had to learn through many painful experiences.

By the time I was in my mid-fifties and met Herb, I had been able to experience enough significant success in my career and personal life to be able to project an image of someone who was confidently strong and self-assured. Too often, though, the energy of sustaining that image took its toll on me, and I would withdraw or shut down my creative energies in order to manage at a barely surviving level. Dissociation was sometimes a serious problem in my younger years. Having learned how to better manage my survival needs as a result of the long recovery from the serious car accident, I met Herb at just the right time to be capable of taking a leap of faith and embracing the opportunity to move into a life of true intimacy, companionship, and friendship with a mature adult who had no room for drama or neediness in his relationships. We made a great team.

One of the best "team plays" we were ever called upon to make occurred at the end of my Ph.D. research. I had taken a circuitous path to arrive at the point where I was ready to defend my dissertation, and Herb had been a crucial support to me in my endeavors. He was so proud to be able to travel with me the long distance to the university where I would be defending, and he was just as devastated as I was, when, in the middle of our journey, as we sat in the airport waiting for our plane, my advisor called me and told me the defense was cancelled.

The long story of that event is worthy of its own space, but what is important for me to say here is that it was one of the worst experiences of my life, and one of the best. I was able to move through the complex channels of resistance, contesting decisions, generating support, and refusing to quit without falling into any one of the old patterns from my younger years. With my advisor's help, the assistance of my committee members, the new internal reviewer, and the original external reviewer, I was able to set effective boundaries, garner help and intervention, and a year later defended a revised version of the dissertation with great success. I learned tremendous lessons from that experience, not the least of which was how to be a better writer.

After the night of the cancelled defense, Herb drove me to his friend's home in Garden River First Nation near Sault Ste. Marie, and there they conducted a Sweat Lodge where I was able to enter in and ask for more help than I had ever asked for before in ceremony. I truly did not want to fail. I wanted a good outcome in a positive way, and, most of all, I didn't want to have to do battle with the "rascal" of shame again. I wanted to be truly and authentically strong and emerge with personal victory and competence—no pretense, no fighting back, no running away, no giving up or shutting down. I was not going to volunteer to be a victim.

I received a gift that I can only consider as coming from Spirit at the feast following the Sweat. This gift of story helped me to center myself in a position of inner strength, knowing and confidence. An elderly woman sat beside me at the table and told me the story. This is how Indigenous wisdom is passed on, in the power of story. She shared the gift of the wisdom that came from her grandmother (I'll call the grandmother Nelda) in a story passed down through her family about the grandmother's experience working as a cook.

Nelda, a very young woman at the time, was hired by a team of guides who worked for railroad surveyors as they laid out lines for the railroad going through the heavy forests in the region around Sault Ste. Marie. This was in the late 1800s, and Nelda's role was to cook for the crew as they travelled through very difficult territory. Following two days of hard work the guides came to a place in the forest where they stopped and said, "We can't go in there. That is badger territory. We have to find another way."

Of course, their words were not greeted with respect and consideration, but instead they were scoffed at, and offered promises of more money, and then, when that didn't change their stance, the white surveyors cruelly threatened them, "If you don't guide us through there we will not only *not* pay you for any of your work, but we'll go back and take the money we have already given to your families. If they starve, they starve. You decide. We have a job to be done and a timetable to keep."

For several hours, they sat at an impasse, the guides and Nelda sitting apart from the angry surveyors, quietly discussing amongst themselves what should be done. Finally, they decided that they could not take food from the mouths of their families. Their community was depending on them to do the work they agreed to do, and they did not want to be denied further opportunities for work in those days. It was hard for their people to get work in a white world. The men decided to go into badger territory. Nelda was only one woman, and even though she could smell the forest odor, which told her it was a mistake to disturb badger territory, and she knew the traditions of her people very well, she had no options but to go along and set up her cooking tent, lay out her supplies, and set to work.

All went well for that night and the next morning. There was no evidence or sound of badgers around, although Nelda felt she was being watched. When the men went out to cut the line for the surveying, she stayed back alone and prepared their lunch, packed up the baskets of food, plates, and eating utensils and walked to the work site. After eating she rested, and then, in the late afternoon, they all walked back together to the camp where she was ready to prepare the evening meal, make tea, and get settled in for another night. But that was not to be.

When the company of surveyors, guides and a solitary woman cook returned to the campsite, it was gone. Completely gone. There was hardly a shred of the camp left, only the large tent poles, the utensils and pots used in the kitchen, a few metal grommets from tents and clothing scattered around, and some metal buttons and belt buckles lying on the ground. The extra boots and shoes, all the food and tea, their blankets and coats, extra clothing, the wooden handles of the knives, the leather of the belts and the canvas of tents, boxes and packs, the matches and tinder, the ropes—*everything* was gone, shredded or disappeared. The surveyors were stunned into silence. Nelda and the guides simply accepted that this was the price they paid for disobeying the Natural Law of the forest and the traditional wisdom of their Elders, and calmly prepared for the group to walk back to Sault Ste. Marie to resupply. The two-day journey without food, shelter or warmth was unpleasant, but the lesson was learned and after that experience, the surveyors carefully consulted the guides and Nelda when difficult decisions needed to be made.

Her story became my own guide through the challenging year after my defense was cancelled. I claimed my "Inner Badger, the Fighter," and took each difficult piece as it came, insisted on completing the dissertation in keeping with what I knew to be my truth and the truth of the research participants whose wisdom I was representing. I relied on the guidance of my advisor, Dr. Gratien Allaire, as well as other academics and First Nations consultants. In the end, I was successful, and the outcome was better than I could have imagined. It was one of the best experiences of my life.

In the years since that time, when I'm feeling particularly vulnerable, I try to remember to consult my "Inner Badger" and remember that wisdom comes in many forms. Lessons can be given by the small and fierce little teachers around us. When the teachings of the smallest ones are disregarded, it is at great risk of an unpleasant outcome. Strength comes with respect. Herb and I often used that metaphor of the "Inner Badger" to encourage each other, or tease each other, as we faced some of our own greatest challenges in the coming year after our journey to the dissertation defense. A little over nine months from that successful defense, Herb passed into the spirit world. I wonder if he encounters the badgers there too.

The cancellation of my original defense was a difficult experience for Herb as well because he felt he'd been personally attacked by the people who had done it. They could not touch him while he was working at the university, but afterward, they could indirectly retaliate by trying to destroy my work. I used an Indigenous research methodology, which some did not want to see inserted into the academy. It was something they had pushed back against in Herb's 23 years of work there. He really struggled in the initial months following my terminated defense. At one point, when I was telling him how frustrated I felt about the experience, I said, "I didn't sign up for this!"

Herb's response showed me just how privileged my little complaints were. "I didn't sign up for this, either! None of us did!" he exclaimed. When he said that I realized he was speaking about everything that the First Nations peoples have experienced because of the direct oppression of their knowledge, their ways of knowing, their way of life in the natural world. Colonization is still alive, and the structural, systemic racism embedded in government, social life, economics, and education continues to drive ongoing genocidal forces and the very destruction of the Earth Herself. So many people still resist this understanding. My experience was an important lesson in teaching me the realities that Indigenous peoples face every day of their lives.

I lived this reality in loving Herb, his family, and his community. I can never think of my life in the same way as I did before. It's as if my Indigenous husband handed me his glasses to put on and look into the realities around me, and I see it through the lens of what he knew and felt and experienced, but not through his eyes, through my own, with a different viewfinder attached. It has changed me and my way of understanding. I have different ways of learning and knowing now. I'm not Indigenous to this continent and cannot feel what he felt, but I was his wife, his companion, his love. I'm a friend, an ally with my own work of decolonization on this continent to pick up and carry. I have a lot of work to do to learn to be a Treaty person. My own ancient "Indigenous spirit" (one of European Indigenous background) is being restored simultaneously with all the responsibilities that this knowledge carries.

Herb shared a story with me once that illustrates the nourishment of Indigenous wisdom. He told me about a day, some years before we met, when he was on his way to a Sweat Lodge ceremony just outside of Sudbury, near Chelmsford. He was driving on a gravel road, winding through the bush north of Sudbury, when he saw a rabbit suddenly dart out in front of him. As Herb slowed the car, a large eagle swooped down over his car, talons outstretched for the rabbit. Just a split second before the eagle would have had its prey in its clutch, Herb saw the rabbit flip over on its back, and, with its powerful hind legs, give a fierce kick at the eagle's chest. The eagle went tumbling into the ditch, then flew up into a tree beside the road, and simply sat there, occasionally shuddering. Herb sat in his car and watched. When the rabbit was long gone, Herb moved on. But still the eagle sat there.

Herb first told me this story as we sat by a sacred fire out in the bush near Burwash Landing. This was the place where we'd been married in a traditional, customary ceremony, marking our sacred commitment to a life together. The place held special memories for us of a joyful time with family and friends. During our first six years together, we often went there to sit and smoke the Pipe and say prayers. It's now regrown into bush with the old road leading to it blocked off. The tepee is gone; the arbor has fallen down, melting into the bushes growing over it. A lone cluster of sage flourishes in a small clearing where sunlight falls. It's been many years since I tried to find the place that lives on in my memory alone. But the memory of the story of the eagle and the rabbit stays with me. I think of it often and of what a rare sight it must have been.

The Spirit of Indigenous teachings, in the manner by which ancient wisdom is transmitted, holds powerful meaning. I sometimes share this story with people who need strength, encouragement, and hope—people who feel helpless, small, weak, and powerless. I sometimes feel that way too. The rabbit teaches how even the prey can fight back and win. The eagle teaches the surprising message that hubris can, in the most unexpected ways, reveal our weaknesses, stop us in our pursuits, and force us to sit still and reflect on our relationships.

I had to learn that in the process of completing my dissertation. I had to be willing to listen to my committee and take their advice on writing. I had to be strong and confident and push back against the people who wanted me to change positions that I could not in good conscience change. I had to remain true to my "data." I had to overcome my fear of powerful people who had more status in the academic world I was attempting to navigate.

The relationship between predator and prey is a powerful mystery. I can't claim to come close to understanding it. But for a brief moment in time, I shared my life with a man who knew this ancient wisdom, the teachings of the Creator, by observing the teachers in nature, and he shared his knowledge the way he knew best, by telling a story. The stories nourish me; they lend a sense of eternity to my existence, a sense of connection to the deeper faith of creation, the love that sustains all of the mystery in one great beauty. In the timelessness of Creation, we are all related.

The West Door

Respect and Reflection

Three o'clock in the morning is not my usual waking time—I'm not a morning person. Sometimes, though, in the early days of our years at Pic River, Herb would find himself awake at that hour. I'm a light sleeper, so I'd hear him moving around in the kitchen, boiling water, making tea, and stirring the cream in with sweetener, clinking the spoon against the cup like a little bell. Since I was awake, I'd get up and make some mint tea and sit with him.

"Is everything okay, sweetheart?" I'd ask.

"Oh, yes, I just have things on my mind." Then we would talk together quietly, rambling around in memories and reflections on various topics, and somehow there was always something to chuckle about or a long comfortable silence, or moments thick with emotions that could bring tears if more words were needed—but they weren't. We understood each other so well. It was a gentle, moving experience when we had those early morning talks, almost as if we were taking a break from time and reality. We would step closer to the Spirit border, that barely perceptible thin line where it might just be possible to reach through to the other side. In that stillness, I sometimes sensed a quivering feeling, as if a vast universe with its silent cloud of witnesses opened up in our peaceful little home—our refuge.

Herb's teachings on the West Door of the Medicine Wheel were that this direction in life is where we learn respect, practice reflection, look twice at the things that trouble or challenge us. He believed this was the direction where souls passed over from physical reality into the spirit world, and that the element of water was represented by this direction. Respect was very important, and his teachings on this are eloquently described in his book, *The Hollow Tree*. Those talks in the early hours of the morning brought us close to the West Door, and its significant lessons.

Many times, the things that weighed on my husband's mind, that woke him up at night and made it impossible to drift back to sleeping and snoring, were things about the past, or the future. Being back in his traditional territory was like being in a place far back in time with relationships and events that cried out for healing. This was a time and place where many things were looked at twice. Here, the real healing could begin, as we were told by his old friend from childhood the first weekend we were in our new home.

We were walking down the road to our house and Claude came by in his big, white, dual-cab pickup truck. He stopped and rolled down the window and called hello to us. We stood there in the brisk spring air and Herb introduced me. Claude said, "I'm glad to see you home, chum. Now the healing can begin." At the time I didn't understand what it all might mean, but it sounded good.

In the early morning talks, I got a glimpse of the level of healing that was at work.

❧

Here's one more thing that told me healing was happening. My husband had a hard time brushing his teeth. For years, his dentist pleaded with him to be more vigilant. It was so hard for Herb to do that, which didn't make sense to me until he said one thing that I immediately understood, "It's about residential school—what they did to me there." I don't know exactly what it was that happened, or if that was the whole reason or a partial explanation, but I understood that for people who have lived with trauma, the smallest things can sometimes trigger a chain of unpleasant emotions, thoughts, and sensory reactions.

I did not comment on teeth brushing after he shared that, but I did notice that after we moved to our new home on Bear Paw Trail, he started to brush his teeth and use mouthwash several times a day. He would occasionally come home from the daily trip into town with new toothbrushes, electric toothbrushes for me and my daughters, dozens of tubes of toothpaste, toothpicks, mouthwash, dental floss and more. When Herb decided something was a good thing, it was always best to have more of a good thing.

The early morning talks were important, nurturing times for our relationship. We were able to explore some things that we usually didn't talk about. Sometimes he'd begin to talk about the teachings and how they helped him, and sometimes I would be the one to remind him of something he'd said that was relevant. This is the way we worked at our marriage, but it never felt like *work*. It wasn't difficult. There were few things that were difficult for us. We used to say we didn't understand why people felt they had to work at something so hard when all it took was love and the Teachings.

One topic we never did reflect on enough was money. I've never had a good handle on money, at least that's what I'd been told by my mother. "Money goes through your fingers like water," she would say. I respected Herb's need to manage his own paycheck and "side money" the way he decided he needed to, but we had similar issues with money going through our fingers "like water."

Before we married, I made a conscious decision never to be in conflict with my husband about money and was quite content to maintain separate bank accounts. It helped me in many ways to maintain my sense of being an independent person, responsible for myself. This decision carried its own consequences, though, and looking back, I wonder if I could have been more helpful to him in this area by approaching it differently. It would have been easy to do in those early morning talks, but, as they say, hindsight is always 20/20.

The whole territory of finances is still not easy for me to navigate—I only do it tolerably well in my life and am occasionally financially insecure for a period of time. I did learn some things, though, in the process of losing everything after my accident, and then, again, in the process of being married to Herb. I learned to trust that there is always enough of everything to do whatever I'm here on this Earth to do. My only task is to do my best, pay my rent, and trust in the benevolence of a limitless universal abundance. I sometimes ponder on the teachings of Jesus in his Sermon on the Mount. They are timeless, too, and focus on generosity, not acquiring wealth. I try to apply these teachings to my life, and to my relationship with money.

Herb was a man who had no sense of money. It was a good thing to have it, and more of it was always better, but when it was gone it was gone, and that was okay too. I didn't have too much of a problem with that. I preferred to keep our finances separate and deal with only my small income and let Herb provide what he wanted to provide and do what he wanted to do with his income. This actually was a very good thing for both of us when it came to tax time. As a dual citizen, I always had to deal with the IRS in the United States in addition to the Canada Revenue Agency, and having separate finances made it easier at tax time for both of us. Making life hard is not the goal of living. Worrying about money makes life hard. It is important to have enough, and that will vary for different people, but chasing after more and more is foolish. It's more important to share.

Herb would tell me funny stories about how his grandfather didn't understand money either but enjoyed getting a big check at the end of the fur season each year when he turned in his pelts and took that big check to the bank. One time, the cash his *Mishomis* received from that check at the bank--where the banker tried in vain to persuade him to leave it--reached a sum of over $6,000. *Nokomis* yelled at *Mishomis* when he got back to their little cabin and made him go back to the bank and leave it there, despite his concern that it would disappear. Herb loved laughing about that, and about the time *Mishomis* got up and walked miles into town to go to the bank, just to make the banker show him the total amount of the actual dollars listed in the bank book. The banker patiently stacked up the bills until they counted $6,000.

Herb told me another story about a man with the same fear his grandfather had. He refused to leave his money in the bank, instead filling mason jars with rolls of bills and burying them at various places out in the bush and near railroad tracks around the small town of White River. Herb said it was still buried out there, dissolved now into dust probably, yet there were occasionally fools who would go looking for it. He himself never looked for it, but he did buy lottery tickets every month, hoping for "found money," and sometimes he actually won a few dollars. He was sure someone had to win, and it might as well be him. That wasn't foolish in his book.

The core ethics of this Elder, though, went bone deep, and he always taught that it was never acceptable to pray for money and wealth when you went into the Sweat Lodge. That was the place for prayer and reflection, the place to go and be as close to the Creator as we can get on this side of eternity. He said it was good to thank the Creator in the Sweat Lodge for all the abundance given so generously to us, but to be greedy and envious, asking for something without giving back, without working for it, was to insult the Creator. Our job on this Earth was to be responsible for ourselves and not expect Creator to rescue us, but to work whenever possible to meet our own needs, and then trust Creator for the rest.

Herb did work hard for his money, and he saved money, but he also spent it generously, and in the last years of his life, unknown to me, he began to lose track of what he had and what he owed. There was no financial benefit left to pass on to his children when he died, except for the tiny on-going royalties from his book. It was what it was, and from a monetized perspective, it could have been better. From my perspective, enough is always enough and the Universe is full of abundance. Our true needs are always met, and the rest is for the lessons we are intended to have, be it financial abundance or the opposite.

Generosity was a core part of Herb's life, and of mine as well. This springs from a desire to have abundance, and to share it abundantly. If someone needed something, Herb never asked questions—he gave with little consideration of the impact on his bank account. He was especially generous to his family, and to me—incredibly so. He gave with no thought of getting it back; he gave remembering the days when he had nothing and people helped him out. When he didn't have it to give, he apologized, and genuinely felt badly that he was broke. "No *shonias*, chum," he would say sadly. He always tried to keep some coins in his pocket for the man or woman on the street who needed it, or the person who needed just a cup of coffee.

Herb respected the power of money. He did understand that it was a medium of exchange that came with the incursion of colonization, and that becoming dependent on money was one of the ways by which power was taken away from the original peoples of the world. Dependency on the money economy had destroyed the gift economy and the sharing that was at the heart of survival for Indigenous peoples. He believed, though, that it was important to respect money and took pride in always being able to pay his rent. To him, that was being responsible. It was "walking the Red Road" to be sure to pay the rent. Herb did not get into political arguments about the term "Red Road" and what it meant. It held a very simple meaning for him—it was *minobimadiziwin*, living the good life.

I heard him respond to someone once who asked him how to "walk the Red Road" by saying, "Pay your rent!" He went on to briefly describe how this spiritual practice, symbolized by the concept of "The Red Road," really implied a basic, simple responsibility for your own life, having a good life, doing what you needed to do to take care of the gift of life, the gift of Nature, given by the Creator.

If a person resented the wealth others had, the destructive resentment would rob them of the opportunity to be self-reliant. He often talked about how the "Old Ones" knew how to work hard and take care of themselves "out there in the bush." He said, "Our ancestors were not lazy. They worked hard!" He did not understand until much later in life that, in the modern world, financial responsibility included also learning how to make your money work for you, such as in the forms of property ownership or investments. Many of us have difficulty with this concept and operate from a deprivation mentality and lose out on being able to make the most of the financial abundance that comes to us.

For the most part, though, money was just there to be enjoyed, used well, and more of it was a good thing because it wouldn't last, couldn't be counted on, and was just temporary—until the next check came in. Herb did okay with his money, though—four years before he died, he had the new house built on his home reserve, where we lived in our own little sanctuary. It was our home together for four short years. He was sad that he'd not been able to completely pay off the mortgage, and one of the last things he asked me to do for him was to check a lottery ticket he had in his wallet. He was quiet and pensive when I came home and teasingly told him, "Not a winner, honey!"

Reflecting on the ways by which Herb respected people, practiced the teachings of the West Door, and tried to walk a good path shows me that I still have a long way to go, a lot left to learn. He never gave me advice directly, just shared his thoughts and ideas, his stories and teachings, and encouraged me to "do what you want to do." When he did give advice to people, it was in response to someone who offered a tobacco gift and asked for specific help on something—a relationship, a job, finances, a move, or anything related to spiritual matters. On one occasion, a person he was acquainted with came to him and offered tobacco in the traditional way and asked for advice about a life-changing event. They invited me to stay as they talked together, and I observed that Herb asked very few questions, listened carefully, and then gave only the minimum of advice.

He said, "The first thing you need to do is take care of the basics. Make sure you do whatever is needed to pay your rent and take care of your basic life needs. After that is taken care of, the rest will come to you." Herb said very little of a serious nature after that, but later, he found out that this person had not taken his advice. He was upset when he learned of the choice they had made and said, "When you give tobacco to an Elder and ask for advice, it is an insult to the Creator to throw that advice away." As far as I know, Herb did not have an opportunity to speak with the person again and did not seek them out and talk about not using the advice they had requested after giving tobacco.

I know that when Herb was working with people in the Sweat Lodge on specific emotional or physical healing needs, he would tell them that once they were healed, it was important to never return to the earlier actions in their life that had caused the problem in the first place. One young person addicted to drugs experienced a dramatic healing in one of his ceremonies, and he instructed them to never use drugs again. He said that doing so would cause sickness, and then if they asked the Spirit for a similar healing, it would not be given. He said that once you were healed, it was an insult to the Creator to go back and do the same old behaviour. Spirit needed respect and right relationship.

Herb held deeply to the belief that practicing the traditional ways was crucial to living a good life, and disrespecting traditions after encountering their power was a dangerous thing to do. I don't know where Herb received his beliefs about this, but most likely in the process of his training and in his personal experiences, he had encountered a truth about how these reciprocal patterns work. When people really want their lives to be different, they do not go backwards after experiencing a breakthrough or a healing.

If they were just "playing at being Indian," as he would sometimes say, or just being what he called "a Hollywood Indian," there was no spiritual respect, no truth to their seeking, and nothing of lasting good would happen. The reciprocity could not flow, could not be activated. In his belief system, people needed to do the necessary reflecting and respecting and use the teachings of the West Door to find healing. He was not interested in "playing games," or acting out an insincere role, pretending to have some magic. He was not a "fake Elder" out to make money from the ceremonies or become famous. He would accept a gift of money or a fee for the time he gave, and the travel and expense of doing the work and providing education or training, but he never charged for a Sweat Lodge ceremony, or for giving a Spirit Name, or for any other sacred ceremony. Gift giving and receiving symbolized reciprocity within a spiritual context, but no amount of money could purchase the value of the ceremony.

People who attempted to engage Herb in insincere endeavors eventually found themselves outside of his sphere of influence. He would not have anything to do with people who wanted to manipulate him for their own self-aggrandizement or benefit. For him, the traditional ceremonies, practices, and teachings were about serious spiritual processes and to disrespect them by not being serious and intentional was truly dangerous. Spirit is not a commodity, and ceremony is not a game or an entertaining and interesting "cultural experience." Spirit is something extremely powerful and not to be played with. Herb knew Creator could help people change the damaging patterns in their lives, but only if they were serious about it. People who were not serious had no business "messing around" with powers they did not understand or respect. He did not want people to use him for their own gain. He did not volunteer to be "a commodity."

Herb told me once that the first thing he had to learn to do after he got sober was "pay the rent." He described his drinking life as a time when very little was taken seriously other than getting the next drink. He did take his graduate school experience seriously enough to practice a form of "harm reduction" by restricting his drinking to weekends only, but as soon as he graduated, all that "harm reduction" went out the window. Life after getting sober, though, was not a lot easier. Because he wanted so much to be healed, to be a good person and to walk in a good way with the Creator, he put into practice the things he was being taught by his

Elders. He did the tedious things they asked him to do, but it took him a long time to put the past behind and live in a new way. He spent the rest of his life striving to correct his mistakes.

After finding sobriety, Herb tried to stop running away from his responsibilities as a father, a role that held great emotional challenges for him. He was able to begin making some good repairs, but it was a journey that continued for the rest of his life, with some unfinished conversations. He was happy about what he had been able to achieve, and he loved and valued each of his children, albeit in different ways.

Herb was an Elder who still worked with his "rascals," and he was dedicated with his whole self to the process of fulfilling the Creator's calling in his life. He wanted more than anything to be able to stand before the Creator with a good heart, having "paid the rent" in his life, having done the necessary "looking twice" and being respectful, and being able to ask in a good way to come into the Creator's home. He truly practiced giving up resentment and would not allow himself to stay angry about things. He couldn't afford to become resentful—his sobriety depended on letting that go.

I like to believe he found the final soul freedom he longed for. He was a good soul who lived the life he was given with every ounce of his being, respecting himself and other people, and loving his Creator and the traditional teachings that had healed him and restored life to him. He shared his knowledge and lived it—he didn't just preach it. He did his walk the best he could, given the knowledge he had. However incomplete the journey may have been on "this side of the camp," he's now free on the other side.

In the last years of our life together, I was often distressed about the job I held at the time. I had difficulty applying the teachings of the West Door to this aspect of my life. Many things about my position frustrated me and I felt undervalued, betrayed, and discounted more often than not. The rewarding work with my clients was a strong personal motivation to persist in trying my best to make a good situation out of a poor position—given my experience, training, and talents. I enjoyed the community I worked in and the co-workers I spent my days with and found that the contact with clients and local physicians was challenging and satisfying. Nevertheless, at the end of the day, I often returned home with complaints to my husband, who was probably tired of hearing them.

I learned not to unload my disappointments on him when his simple comment, "Annie, I just want you to be happy," became his standard response to my distress. It was a comment that was so quiet and simple that I had to stop and reflect on what I was doing, not only to myself but also to him. Allowing work unhappiness to intrude on our happy life was a waste of the precious time we had together.

His wish for me to be happy was a reminder of an observation he once made about my cultural heritage in our early years together. I had explained to him my analysis of the history behind some of the family and community problems I saw and experienced in the Mennonite world, and he commented, "I think that Mennonites suffer from a 'Suppression of Happiness Disorder.'"

It was like a flash of light into a deep fog when he said that. Of course! What I had absorbed from my cultural background became transmitted to me as subtle messages that my happiness was last on the list of things to think about, and probably should not be on the list at all. Instead, what was important on the list was self-sacrifice to help or please others.

I remember one event from an experience I had as a seven-year-old, enthusiastic little girl, when I asked my mother if I could bring some flowers I loved to the church. I thought that the beautiful yellow daffodils of spring would look so pretty on a windowsill in the barren church meeting room, but my mother told me I had to ask permission from the minister first. I shyly went to him and told him I wanted to bring my new spring flowers to church and was somberly scolded for asking that. I will always remember his serious tone of voice as he said, "Remember that little dog who ran into the church last week? If you brought flowers they would be just as distracting to everyone! In church we are to be quiet and serious and think about God, not flowers, or puppies." The memory of the shame I felt and how he laughed at me then has remained as a sour memory. Somehow, I received the message that my enthusiasm and happiness and simple childlike joy in nature was not acceptable, and it followed that I, too, was not acceptable, but shameful. I see it now as an example of how the intergenerational suppression of happiness seeped into even the smallest aspects of life with no awareness of where it came from.

As I engaged in my research for my degree, I learned even more about this 'Disorder' and delved once again into rereading *Martyrs Mirror*, a book that is second only to the Bible in many Mennonite and most Amish households. I began to understand the origins of this 'Disorder' and how it was shaped by the religious and political environment of the 16th and 17th-centuries in Europe. The dominance of the Roman Catholic Church, the Inquisition, and the intrusion of the State Church system into the minutiae of people's lives created deep intergenerational wounds. Reading *Martyrs Mirror* gave me a view of how long the torture now known as "water boarding," has been around. It was used by the Inquisitors in interrogation of their victims. Sexual torture was a routine part of the Inquisition, all under the direction of the Church and sanctioned by the military power of the State. The institutionalization of this type of violence has had an effect that has tumbled down through the centuries into my life.

The poison of that wounding came to Turtle Island, and the damage of institutionalized violence in a racist society continues. In the 1500s and 1600s, even laughter was condemned in certain religious circles. Mennonite children were instructed not to laugh but to be sober and serious and pious. Their parents were being imprisoned and executed by the thousands. Even adolescents were executed for their beliefs. Anabaptist children were given to other families, yet normal, healing play was denied to them—only prayer was acceptable and allowed. The culturally ingrained trauma responses from that era have seeped deep into the psyche of Anabaptist descendants, the traditional ethnic Mennonite and Amish peoples, many of whom unknowingly pass on intergenerational trauma to this day.

Through the restoration of the traditional teachings in his life, Herb was able to fight back against those wounding forces. He was able to restore the spark of his spirit into a life of *Minobimadiziwin*, and he took great joy in the relief of the transformation. He lived in hope but had a realistic understanding of how much work needed to be done. He would not allow discouragement about social injustice to rob him of his serenity and happiness. He loved the good things in his life, avoided poison like alcoholic drink, laughed easily, slept well, enjoyed good food and good company, lived a balanced life and stayed in the here-and-now.

How refreshing and enlightening it was to live with a person who not only knew how to take responsibility for his own happiness, but also how to gently and strongly insist that I take responsibility for my own happiness as well. I now value it and treasure it and nurture it. Herb's own healing from the trauma of genocide and intergenerational damage was hard-won, and he loved his life and lived it to the fullest with joy and self-confidence. I learned so much about happiness in my ten years with him. My biggest fear following his death was that I might forget how to be who I had become with him. I liked the "me" that I was with Herb!

The bequest Herb left me are his words, "I just want you to be happy. I love you so much." I hold fast to my determination to claim my own happiness as I continue a good and purposeful life in the years that I have left to live without him. It's his memory, his spirit presence, which gives me happiness now, even though it will always be tinged with sadness from missing the special human being he was in my life. All human beings have to face this at some point—I know I'm not alone or unique in that way. I know now that I can create a new life for myself and be happy and still feel his presence even though he is not physically here. I know now that the love we shared can be expanded in the years I have ahead. Love is not ended. Life wants to live and love wants to love.

ॐ

During the six years we lived in Sudbury, I was not only working on an interdisciplinary Ph.D. in Human Studies, but I was also working on completing my four Fasts (one each year for four years) for the Pipe, which had been gifted to me in 2008 by Herb and several other elders at the Garden River Healing Lodge, near Sault Ste. Marie, ON. During fasting times, Herb would come to the fasters out in the bush once a day, sit with us around the sacred fire, smoke the Pipe with us and share teachings. The third year of this four-day experience was the most difficult one for me. On this particular Fast, Herb emphasized the teachings of the West Door, and asked the fasters to do some deep reflection on our lives, the positive and negative side of things in our lives. He asked us to respect our "rascals," to "look twice" and approach them as "teachers," and said that to not look at these shadow sides of our inner life would prevent us from finding our vision.

The concept of "the rascals" addresses the negative aspects on the Medicine Wheel. *Inferiority*, feeling you are less than others, is the rascal in the East Door—the direction of vision, good food, and new beginnings. *Envy*, wanting something without working for it, is the rascal in the South Door—the direction of time and relationships. *Resentment*, hanging on to bad feelings, is the rascal in the West Door—the direction of reflection, self-examination, and looking at things twice. *Not-caring* (apathy), not being willing but being willful and selfish, is the rascal in the North Door—the direction of caring, wisdom, and movement. *Jealousy*, craving to control that which belongs to someone else, is the rascal at the centre of the Medicine Wheel—the direction of Mother Earth, or ME, which also stands for oneself. Herb used to say it is the distorted drive to control someone else that is at the root of all domestic violence, along with inferiority. People who use power and control, and are violent with their partner and children, avoid the work of self-control, humility, and love. They have lost their vision, and their spirit.

The night before Herb gave us these teachings, as I lay alone in my little tent underneath the tall pine trees listening to the wind, my body began experiencing the natural effects of going without water and food for two days. I drifted in and out of slumber and visited the outhouse frequently to deal with bouts of diarrhea and eventually moved to sit beside the sacred fire to wait for morning, where Herb found me when he came up the trail at first light. He seemed genuinely shocked to see the state I was in and said, "Annie! I'm taking you out of this Fast right now!" I told him no, I wanted to finish the last day, but he was distressed by the look on my face and asked me what was happening. I began to weep and shared with him that whenever I closed my eyes, or looked at the fire, I could see people burning.

"Annie, those are your ancestors, the ones you told me about who were persecuted so long ago," he said. "They have a message for you. Listen!"

Herb had me drink some cedar water, and took some other ceremonial steps to help me, and I went on to successfully complete the fast. (Seven months later, I, my brothers, and our children faced the impending death of our 95-year-old family matriarch. It would be another two years before I could complete my fourth and final Fast). At the end of the third Fast, after our Sweat Lodge and the Feast, I went home with Herb to our apartment, showered, and went to bed early after drinking copious amounts of herbal tea.

That night, I had a dream that has been a guiding force in my life since that time. It was a dream that confirmed for me the truths I was encountering in my experiences through the ceremonies and left me with a message from my ancestors so clear in my mind that it has never faded. They intensely communicated to me the importance of what I do with my life here on Mother Earth, and how intimately it's connected with the work they continue to do on the other side: *"If you do not do your work there, we cannot do what we are meant to do here!"*

I'm still, all these years later, reflecting on the meaning of that dream, working to respect the inner knowing that I have, welcoming the connections I have with those who have passed on, and striving to carry forward what is mine to carry as I live out my life. The memory of my life with my partner, my husband, my friend, helps me to go deeper into my spiritual life. I am inspired to work towards balance, to nurture my spirit, and to continually let go of that "Suppression of Happiness Disorder" I inherited. I feel supported to be open to a new life ahead.

Although I don't always succeed at the level I would like, and sometimes fall back into complaining, or experience episodes of resentment, I strive to stay thoughtful and strong with the insights I have, the things I have learned, and the ideas that arise from my experiences in life. I try to share what I know in as many ways as I know how. I'm always aware that my "rascals" keep trying to interfere with my path and also know that they are trying to teach me to walk well, to stay balanced and keep moving forward, to pay attention, to respect myself and my Creator and the gifts I've been given.

It's a good road to walk. Along the way, I'm learning the lessons that bereavement teaches, the lessons of financial challenges, and the lessons that not having a permanent home hold for me. Some people seem to expect me to have things all figured out, to be a person who is always calm and settled, confident, and hopeful, but I'm not always able to express those characteristics of mine. Sometimes those qualities are sitting on the back shelf of a closet somewhere. Many times, I feel the way I expressed to my daughter one day, "I'm not the Yoda Mama! I'm the Yoda Mama without any skin left!"

I can't always be who people want or need me to be, but I can be my real self, and I can say honestly, "What you see is what you get." Know that what you see in me will be different from day to day because I'm a growing human being. What you see may be a projection of your own need and not who I truly am. Take some time to respect, to reflect, to listen, and learn. We are the mirror for each other, the gift to each other. We are enough—we are all that is needed to be love for each other.

THE NORTH DOOR

CARING

When Herb turned to the traditional ways of his ancestors to heal from the ravages of alcoholism and the wounds of historical trauma, he did more than add something to what he knew about getting through life. He completely changed the foundations of his life, the core principles by which every aspect of his life was directed.

This did not happen overnight, and I met him after he'd had decades of practice, learning from mistakes and fine-tuning the essential paradigm of knowledge that guided his choices. I did not know him through the worst years of his struggle to grow, change, and heal—I knew him in the final stage of the life of an Elder, when he was consolidating his gains, making peace with all that was past, and learning the final lessons in his life before going to be with his Creator. He shared this richness with me generously.

The teachings of *"The Little Boy"* contained the framework of his philosophy of life and encompassed the lessons of the Medicine Wheel. Other teachings were also important: The Five Colors of the Medicine Wheel, The Seven Grandfather (Wisdom) Teachings, The Four Levels of Knowledge Above the Ground, The Teachings of the Pipe and the Feather, among others. These core teachings informed all that he did, all of who he was, and all that he wished to carry forward in his life as he strove to live the traditions of the Cree and the Anishnaabeg peoples. He was never about proselytizing, but rather about sharing with respect and integrity. The transformation that took place in his life long before we met was profound and awe-inspiring; but all that said, he was still a very human man trying to be as close to the Creator as he could and to do the best with what he had.

The teachings of the North Door are about caring. The "rascal" of this direction is 'not caring,' or apathy and despair. Applying these teachings could be called pedagogy in academic language, but for Herb, that would simply have meant the practical application of "how" to do the "what." He talked often about the long distance from the head to the heart and expressed sadness and frustration that so many people could hear him share a teaching and continue to be clueless about how to apply it in their own lives. Caring, for him, meant the active application of efforts to live in harmony as much as possible in this world, always aware that Creator and Mother Earth intended life to be good, and intended for people to care about all of creation, including their own.

Whenever Herb gave a lesson on the North Door, he gave examples of how the natural world demonstrates caring. He would say something like this:

> *When North Wind comes in late autumn, this north part of the world is covered by a white blanket of snow. The color for this direction is white, and the people represented in this direction are the Caucasian people. The lesson here is about movement; the air moves things. Experience teaches us that the cold north wind and the snow move us to seek shelter to keep from freezing so it is teaching us to care about survival, the lesson for this direction—caring. The 'Grandfather,' or the spirit animal, the dodem, that sits in the north direction is the bear. The Elders tell us the bear is the ultimate healer. She heals all physical illnesses, mental illnesses, and spiritual illnesses, and is the great protector. We are also told that when the bear hibernates in the wintertime, she prays for all the red people in the East, she prays for all the Asian people in the South, she prays for all the black people in the West, and prays for the white people in the North. The bear prays for peace in all the directions—world peace. The bear does that work for us every winter. We thank the bear in our ceremony for this work and thank the bear for helping us to find peace within ourselves. The bear is a very powerful spirit animal that works with all of humanity.*

Herb gave examples of caring in nature, such as the caring the loon shows for its mate and its young, the affection that horses and dogs and other animals show to each other and with other species. He talked about how the first cries of a baby are the first demonstration that the baby human knows how to care for itself by calling out for help from the caregivers. The baby wants to be fed and warm, wants to be cleaned, to be held and comforted, and taught how to be a human being. The traditions say that while children are still in the spirit world, they choose their parents, their caregivers. The children are the teachers of the parents as much as the parents and the clan are teachers for the children. Herb learned how to bring caring into his life by practicing these traditional lessons from the Elders, and he actively worked to care for himself and others as long as he was alive.

I find it profoundly healing to think of caring in this fashion. Caring is an action, not a feeling. It's generated by natural impulses to honor the self, and to honor the Creator. Caring is not just an idea, or something one *should do* in order to obey a higher authority, nor is it a transactional effort of exchange to get something or manipulate someone into doing or believing a certain thing. I'd been taught in my life that caring was something we were *supposed to do* because "God loved us first, therefore we must love others." That implied we should try to show people how "Jesus saved" them. The teachings I had received about Jesus telling us to love others as we loved ourselves were confusing to me because I had also absorbed the idea that loving myself was not important. The evangelistic mantra, "God first, others next, myself last," had become ingrained in me unconsciously through my childhood experiences.

I doubt that the family and culture in which I grew up purposefully intended to deprive me of good feelings about myself and create in me such profound confusion and mystification, but the end result of what I absorbed was low self-esteem, and not caring for myself, not feeling free to devote personal action to the ideas and dreams I had for myself. My career interests were shaped toward professional social work because I received praise from people about my abilities to help others. Following my passions for things I wanted to learn about in art and writing was not nurtured in the same way.

When I was just a little girl, my mother said to me, "Annie, I don't know how you do it, but you know everyone in the neighborhood and exactly what their problems are!" I also felt good when I experienced tangible positive results from my caring efforts, and I loved learning all that I did in the process of my professional training. Much of it helped me form a foundation for caring for myself, but my true inner dreams of creativity took a back seat for most of my life. I acted in transactional ways more than I realized, believing I, and others, could get things from each other by acting certain ways.

The ingrained impulses I struggled with were the impulse to "people-please" and strive for approval, which negatively affected my development and adult life. Of course, these impulses also protected me to some extent, and led to accomplishments and fulfilling ambitions, but at a cost to my true self. The natural teachings of the Elders went a long way to turning that around. It was a large gift of caring that I received from Herb, and we were able to always show caring and respect toward each other.

Herb's ready smile and cheerful, "Hello, lovey!" each morning set the stage for trust to flourish between us as I grew to rely on him and see his care for me as predictable and consistent. I knew he "had my back" to an extent no one else had ever shown. He would sometimes tell me, "Annie, I would go to the wall for you. I would lay down my life for you." This was something I didn't quite understand. No one ever said anything like that to me before or demonstrated that in any way. I learned to recognize it as his way of deeply expressing his love for me, and his commitment to our life together. The deep abandonment and betrayal I had experienced in my childhood and first marriage were healed in my heart by the relationship we nourished together. It's my responsibility to still work on the scars, but now I know it *is* possible to heal, to be happy.

Humans will naturally express caring for themselves first, and if the lesson is learned in a healthy way, a human will naturally learn how to care for others, the Creator, and Mother Earth— all of Creation—as part of the whole process and action of caring. This is the way humans learn joy and how to be happy and love the life they have. This is healthy, and love flows for one's family and the larger community from this abundance. If children are not shown safety, predictability, and love, they will not learn to love and trust, regulate their emotions, and manage distress. When humans are wounded in the area of caring, everyone suffers, and many dysfunctional aspects of society emerge.

One of the first things I noticed when I moved to Herb's apartment in Sudbury was the big blue box for recycling, just inside the apartment door. He tried to be careful about recycling, and he directly related that to the teachings he had about the North Door. Caring for Mother Earth was tangibly activated by recycling as much as possible. Herb truly valued caring for Mother Earth. As he aged, he was increasingly distressed by the damage being done to the Earth by modern economic forces and careless people.

Climate change interested Herb and he often purchased books about the subject. The work that Al Gore was doing regarding climate change fascinated him, and watching David Suzuki's programs on television captivated him. He told me a story of meeting David Suzuki once a long time ago in an establishment in Toronto. David told him he had originally wanted to be a doctor. Herb joked about that, saying, "Here he was, an environmentalist doing so much, and he still talked about wanting to be a doctor!" I jokingly reminded him that here he was, a respected Anishnaabe Elder and a university professor, and he still sometimes talked about having wanted to be a truck driver. We shared a good laugh about that.

Herb wanted to write a book about climate change from the Medicine Wheel perspective. He made efforts in that direction several times over the last five years of his life but was never able to get out exactly what he wanted to say. I promised him that, after my dissertation was completed and I graduated, I would put my own writing aside and help him to write his book. Soon after I received my diploma, we began that project together. Eight months later, while we were waiting for a diagnosis of what was causing his health problems, we had a phone conversation with Heather Campbell, the publisher who was excited about being able to publish his second book.

I will always remember that phone conversation. It was February 21, 2016, about 7:00 in the evening, already dark outside, and snowing. Herb was sitting in his most comfortable chair with a warm blanket over his lap, and the speakerphone made a three-way conversation easy. About 15 minutes into the conversation, I noticed that Herb had suddenly fallen asleep, and I took the phone off speaker and talked to Heather myself.

"I think if the book is going to be completed, you and I will need to work together to help him get down what he wants to say. Is that something you can work on with us?" I asked her. She assured me that would be possible, and I told her we would be in touch, but I never imagined at the time that the project of Herb's second book would not have time to materialize.

The next day, Monday, February 22, about 2:00 in the afternoon, I received a phone call at my office from Herb's doctor. She said calmly, "Annie, I'd like to give Herb some information on the phone, and I wanted to know when you would be able to go home and be with him while I talk with him."

Those were ominous words, especially considering that we had been waiting for weeks to get some answers to his perplexing medical problems, which had shown up all of a sudden while we were on a cruise that January. The cruise was on his bucket list because he *really* wanted to take me to the Bahamas, even though I wasn't particularly in favour of going on a cruise. It seemed to be an extravagance we didn't need just then, and when he became very ill on the trip, I felt my premonitions had been correct—something not very good was happening.

As if from a faraway place, I heard the doctor's voice on the phone. "Would you like to hear what I have to tell him before you go home?"

I burst into tears and said, "Tell me now, so I can deal with my feelings before I have to help him deal with this." That's when she informed me that there was a mass in my husband's liver, all further tests had been cancelled, and an appointment was being scheduled with the oncologist. When I left my office that afternoon, I knew I would not be returning for a long time. I was extremely distressed on the 20-minute drive home, and as I turned from the TransCanada Highway onto the road back toward Pukaskwa National Park and home at *Biigtigong Nishnaabeg,* I felt as if I were turning to enter a different life. Part of my mind knew what was coming, what all of this meant, but I was already beginning to detach, to distance myself, to "stay in my head" as a way of protecting myself, and even the scenery of the snowy forest I drove through looked different to my eyes. A sense of unreality settled around the familiar sights, and the dim light of the overcast afternoon felt fitting for what I was driving toward.

Thus, we began the journey into "that good night." All my own personal feelings took a back seat during that time, occasionally breaking through into powerful emotions, but I hid that from Herb. I put effort into staying on top of all that needed to be done, learning as much as I could about the metastasizing cancer that was taking my husband from me. Unconsciously, I acted as if this could keep me ahead of the impending loss I knew was coming. I knew it would not be a long journey, but I did not know that day after the phone call with Heather that we would see Herb pass over into the Spirit world a brief two and a half weeks later. I had no idea what lay ahead for me in the months and years after that. I did not realize the level of caring that would become necessary.

Now, traveling on alone without my companion, I reach deep into the teachings he left me to learn how to navigate with caring through the grief that comes with such a loss. A quote from G. H. Lewes exemplifies what I have tried to do since then: "The only cure for grief is action." The actions of caring for myself have been my primary focus since his death, as well as caring for family and friends as best as I am able. I haven't been able to be perfect in that caring, but my intentions are solid. I had dealt with loss and grief before, but I truly did not understand a thing about grieving and mourning until my husband died.

Learning to care for myself and continue on in the good life while holding on to the person I wanted to be has challenged me deeply. After he died, one of Herb's close friends said to me, "Your healing will come in solitude," and I recognize that truth now that I've had time to really be alone. Solitude is a comfort more often than not, but Herb's physical absence in my life creates a solitude unlike any I've ever known before. It's difficult to put into words the depth of this aloneness, which can be both blessing and burden. I'm striving to understand aloneness as a gift, and to allow the lessons of this gift to change me for the better.

As a child I'd been shamed, scolded, and punished for crying and felt a deep shame whenever I shed tears. I was a child with strong emotions who cried easily, and the punishment for crying didn't help end my tears. After my accident, the location of the core brain injury meant that I, again, cried easily, similar to post-stroke patients. I wept about almost anything—puppies, TV commercials, not being able to find my toothbrush, remembering something sad—and it was difficult to learn strategies to control those tears. Now, again, I was suddenly in touch with my tears and the feelings of discomfort were back. I cringed at the bouts of weeping that I could not control.

In the years with Herb, I hardly ever cried. After he died, it seemed like I cried all the time. Even now, years later, I cry when the memories come up and seem unable to stop the flow of tears. For a while, I isolated myself from other people because I was afraid I wouldn't be able to control my tears in front of them. Eventually, I pushed through that fear and engaged in strategies to work on controlling my tears, much as I had done after the accident. I realize that some of my tears are about things that I pushed out of my mind during the weeks my husband was dying.

When Herb was so sick and dying, I never allowed myself to share my tears with him. He never saw me cry. I guess I thought I was being strong for him, fulfilling my caregiving commitment, but in reality, I was trying to avoid facing the pain of his loss. I was trying to deny that what was happening was full of sorrow, for both of us, and for our families, and I did not want to talk about that with him. I was afraid of my tears, afraid of the emotional pain, afraid of the messy upheaval the cancer was causing in our life together. I did not want to accept that I was losing my life, too, losing our life together as I had known it. I did not care enough to go deep into this process and find ways to share that loss with him; or maybe I cared too much and mistakenly thought I was helping him by avoiding this. I saw him being so strong for his friends and family, and I didn't want to burden him with one more heavy responsibility to comfort me.

Because the cancer had spread from his liver to his lungs, kidney, and spine, it was difficult for Herb to breathe in the last weeks of his life. He did not experience excruciating pain and only used a few very low doses of morphine. His abdomen became terribly distended, so a permanent port was placed to drain fluid, to try to keep him more comfortable, but that in turn became an irritation to manage, which both of us had to cope with. He was very patient and dignified through it all, never complaining or lashing out, remaining calm and philosophical about what was happening. He slept more and more, but was always delighted to receive visitors or phone calls, and then the fatigue would take over and he would need solitude and quiet, resting for long hours. Not everyone understood his need, and mine, for rest and time alone. I was fiercely protective of his need for solitude.

The grace and dignity that Herb demonstrated through all those days was inspiring to all of us who loved him so much. He interacted with his Personal Support Workers, the hospice nurses, and his doctor with kindness and humor, and comforted his friends. I overheard him say on the phone to one of his oldest and dearest friends, "I'm okay with this, chum. I'm ready to go. The Creator is a good, kind Spirit and we all go home someday." It was only with his sister and his aunt that he was able to express the regret of what he was leaving, and what he wished he could still do. They were the ones to whom he said, "I hate to leave Annie." He wanted months, not days, but he accepted what was. "It is what it is," was one of the things he would often say, and this philosophy served him well in the end.

One afternoon I said to him, "Sweetheart, is there anything that you'd like to talk about?"

His reply was given calmly, with a sweet, sad smile. "Maybe later, lovey." Then we hugged, and he soon dropped off to sleep. It was my only attempt to cross my barrier of fear. I've often wondered since what he might have been able to say had he not felt so protective of me.

Because of the difficulty breathing, he was not able to use his Pipe, or burn sage or sweetgrass for smudging, so I didn't talk with him about that either, which I feel sad about now, because losing touch with the traditional items that were important to him in his spiritual practices must have been very difficult. Because he could no longer keep his balance and walk and had little strength, he was not able to complete the last Sweat Lodge he had wanted to do and, again, I didn't talk with him about that. He expressed concern that taking care of him was too hard for me, but I would not talk with him about that either, thinking that I was helping him by reassuring him, by insisting that we would stay at home and not go to the hospital, and that I would do all in my power to keep him comfortable in his own home if that was what he wanted. It was my pride speaking, because I had at one time confided in a close friend that I was afraid I would not be up to the task of taking care of him when things got really hard. Going to the hospital would have felt like defeat, failure, surrender to the cancer. Staying home felt safe, familiar, comfortable, and I wanted that for him more than anything.

Enough Light for the Next Step | 111

When Herb said, "I hate to leave Annie," he didn't say it to me because he sensed that I did not want to talk about his leaving. Although over the years we had spoken together of our wishes regarding end of life things, when it actually came to pass, we were in unspoken agreement to not talk about what was happening. This "don't talk rule" was a pretty powerful one when our backs were against the wall. I realize now that the tears that overwhelm me are about the unfinished conversations that I must attend to in order to mourn and recover from his loss and continue with caring for myself. Herb would not want me to stop caring about my life. He wants me to be happy—to enjoy *minobimadiziwin*.

The body deteriorates at the end of physical life, and along with the normal distancing that occurs in this dying process, it seemed this ending was conspiring together with our need to care for each other and protect each other to result in an unspoken solution—to not speak about what was happening. This contributed to an excessively rapid closure of the greatest event in our lives. Herb's death came quicker than anyone thought it would. We were all prepared—the medical care givers and the family—to be engaged in this dying process for months, not weeks. If we had had more time, would we have been able to speak together about what was happening? Of course, there's no way to answer that question, but what I've been left with is the task of completing the inner conversation and learning how to care for myself in the process, continuing to keep the fire alive in myself.

In our life together, Herb and I never said "Goodbye" to each other. It was always something along the lines of, "See you later, lovey," or, "So long—I'll be back," or "Bye, honey, I love you." Even when he was leaving this world, we didn't say "goodbye" to each other. I think it was a reluctance on both our parts to acknowledge the imminent final departure, and also an acknowledgement of the connection we felt to each other. The bond we had was not brittle—it was something timeless that could stretch for thousands of miles and weeks at a time. Our whole-heart connection was about something greater than who we were as individuals. It was rooted in Spirit. We were individuals not owned by the other and free to come and go as we needed. We completely supported the other in meeting whatever needs there were to travel or go someplace alone. Our bond was not a clinging type of connection.

There's another aspect of the "Goodbye" issue as well, and it's cultural. The way Anishnaabeg acknowledge a parting in the language is generally signified by the phrase, "*Baa maa pii*." Sometimes I heard just the simple phrase, "*Baa maa*." Other times, I heard the phrase, "*Giwaabamin, baa maa pii minwa*." I understood it to mean that "we would see each other after a while." I was also told many times that there was no language equivalent meaning "goodbye" in his language. The word was itself somewhat suspect, alien, with a negative connotation, indicating the ending of something as opposed to a continuation of a relationship with an absence. Perhaps that's only a misunderstanding on my part, but I do understand that this concept of "saying goodbye" is something that did not exist in Anishnaabeg culture prior to contact with the European dominant cultures.

I had always understood "goodbye" as something said whenever people were parting. If I gave any thought to its true meaning, I considered it to originate from Old English, indicating something along the lines of, "God go with you on your way as you go by." Where I absorbed that understanding I have no idea—perhaps from vague, distorted memories of high school English classes with a teacher who was fond of the Old English language. Growing up, I often heard "*Auf wiedersehn*," a German phrase that roughly translates to "I will see you later," although it was not in my daily vocabulary since I never learned to fluently speak that particular ancestral language.

I had no desire to say "goodbye" to the man I wanted in my life. I wanted him to be with me for a while. We had plans for retirement. I would stop working in 2017 and then we were going to do the quintessential Canadian thing of being "snowbirds," spending the winter months in the southern United States. We were going to visit the other provinces, and maybe go on another cruise, this time to Alaska. To see our dream retirement suddenly and abruptly come to an end was bitter.

I did not want to say goodbye to the dream. I did not want to say goodbye to my life as I knew it. I did not want to say goodbye to Herb.

When Herb took his last breath, I was so shocked at how quickly this reality was upon us that it never occurred to me to whisper either "goodbye" or "*Giwaabamin, baa maa pii*" or even "*gizhaagien*" (I love you). At the moment when the last deep sigh left his body, I said, "Can this really be? Am I really seeing my husband take his last breath?" I was unbelieving, astounded, in awe, stunned. It was like watching someone being born, and I didn't get to be part of it—I was left alone.

In the months afterward, I would allow myself to imagine he'd just gone back to visit Argentina or some distant place and would be home soon. I listened for the sound of his car in the driveway, even though I knew I'd returned it to the leasing dealership in Wawa. When I woke alone in the morning, I imagined he was just in the kitchen fixing coffee for us. When someone walked on the porch, I would have an instant thought, "Herb is home!"

Herb was home—with his Creator. But I still wanted him here with us. None of us in either of our family networks were ready to let him go. We were not ready to think that the preciousness of Herb was gone from our sight. We all, to one extent or another, still wanted to warm our hearts by the fire with him. We still needed his wisdom and guidance and support to give us strength, to help us move forward with the teachings and learn to be wise and caring.

Yet the conversation continues, and more often now I find myself whispering to his spirit, "*Baa maa pii, gizhaagien.*" I understand now that it's just a thin veil between our spirits. I'll see him later, after a while, and the "I love you" will come as easily as ever. He's just gone from my sight for now. In the years when he traveled internationally, teaching or doing ceremonies, I did not accompany him, so I had time to get used to long absences, which did not disrupt our relationship. The permanence of this separation here in the physical realm is more challenging for me to handle, but I know his spirit continues to be part of my life.

The North Door is the place for Elders. Herb taught that after our middle years during the West Door teachings, we would move to the North Door to become wise elders and carry forward the teachings and care for the youth, feed their fire to help them with their vision, their relationships, and the hard work of walking the Red Road. I wanted to have more time with Herb in this direction, but it was his time now to travel on, to go home, and I had to find a way to accept that and adapt to a life without his physical presence.

Herb often talked about "the fire" within each of us, which the Creator has placed there, and which is our responsibility to care for.

His teachings were based in his understanding of the Medicine Wheel knowledge:

> *At the centre of the Medicine Wheel there is a 'fire', at the heart of Mother Earth. When we build a sweat, we start with a fire to heat the 'grandfathers'—the stones that are collected and heated to take into the Lodge with us to share their strength with us and help heal us. That sacred fire we start with represents the Creator, and also the fire in our hearts. When we pray in the lodge, we send prayers in the direction of the fire in the sky world, the Creator's fire, the sun, and also the fire in our hearts and the fire at the centre of the Earth. These fires align to provide perfect balance, to find a way to understand how to heal the Earth. The center of the Medicine Wheel also represents Mother Earth, Shkagamik-Kwe, and the colour for the direction of this centre is green, a colour of life.*

This teaching on the fire is like a metaphor, a story about how to care for ourselves and for Mother Earth. It's an ancient, abstract, and poetic way to express an overarching truth that humans need to have at the core of their lives—the truth of balance. Without a balanced view of ourselves as humans in a natural world, we will over-exploit the resources Mother Earth gives. Humans are currently living in a terrible time of climate change, and in the sixth largest extinction era the planet has ever known.

The ancient prophecies also reveal that now is a time of great shift, and great opportunity for either mortal disaster or transformation. The metaphor of a balance between the fire at the heart of Mother Earth, our own inner heart fire, and the fire of the sun, can be seen as an inspiration to work to care for the Earth, to strive to be in a right relationship with the Earth, with ourselves, and with each other. Herb knew about this, he felt deeply about this, and he tried hard to talk about it with other people whenever he had the opportunity.

When we talked together about the environmental concerns that weighed heavily on Herb's heart, he talked about the colour green and how it represented Mother Earth, and how we need to remember to care for Her. He believed if humans didn't soon learn how to care better for Mother Earth, matters would be taken into Her own powers. He talked about how taking responsibilities seriously in the North Door direction means that human society will focus on caring for Mother Earth's resources and not exploiting Her for an extraction economy. The work Herb did for his community in the last several years of his life included serving on the Band Council and working with the Lands and Resources Committee. His greatest passion was for his community to achieve self-governance so it could progress in reclaiming this responsibility to care for the Earth sustainably.

Early in his tenure at his home Reserve, Herb got involved in community matters, helping to provide leadership in a key area close to his deepest concerns for the Earth. He sent a letter to the Band Manager regarding his concerns about the environment:

> *I would like to suggest stronger consideration to the food security of the community. Land and food are at the heart of what it means to us to be Aboriginal people. The past development and industrialization in our territories has not given sufficient attention to the negative impact on our people's land and food. Things have become disrupted and contaminated in many places and the habitat of many species has been eroded. That affects our traditional hunting and fishing. We need to consider an integrated approach to improving how we deal with all of this as future pressure on our resources grows. All the areas of the report—environment, biological, socio-economic, physical and cultural, and land, water and resource use—are linked. They cannot be divided one from the other. It all has to be considered together with no one part diminished. That way our future of food security stays balanced. So, in all of these areas something needs to be acknowledged regarding food security. What would this community do, in the near or far future, if the one highway (17) and the rail tracks would be interfered with or closed? No boats are going to bring in food. And if the natural world around us has been so damaged it can't support the animals and plants, how could we go out in the bush and find a way to*

feed our families? We don't know how many days or weeks we could survive on empty store shelves. We need to think about this and prepare, and [-----] in its development must take all this into account.

If you would like more information about food security issues for Aboriginal people in Canada you could look at some of the [internet] sites I have been looking at for food security.

There is also a recent visit to some of the Reserves by the commissioner from the UN and he expressed the concerns he had about the hunger he saw among Indigenous peoples in Canada. The Federal Government dismissed what he said and didn't accept his report, and they've gotten a lot of criticism for that. Let's hope the [-----] people and the other ones who want rights to our resources will pay more attention than the government. But we have to lead them and let them know how important this is to our identity and survival.

Thank you, Herb Nabigon

When I look back at that time in our lives, what stands out to me was how deeply Herb felt the need to lead people in his community to care for their land, their territory, and look at the natural world and the challenges it faced. He directly linked it to ultimate survival. Sometimes, he would say to me, "I'm tired. I've done my work. Let the younger people work on this," and then go out the next day or week to yet another meeting, yet another conversation with people regarding the land, the territory, and the responsibility for self-governance and self-direction. The key words were responsibility and survival. We had easy times in our home together in those last years, taking walks on the beach with our dog, enjoying dinner together, watching the evening news and maybe a movie before bedtime. Most of the time, Herb was a real news junkie—he turned on the TV every time he was in the house. Other times he sat in silence, looking out the window with a calm and peaceful look on his face. Either way it went, if I came and sat with my cup of coffee in the mornings and started to discuss some deep, philosophical idea, he would sometimes turn to me with a gentle smile and say, "Oh, Annie. It's too early in the morning to have such a deep discussion. Let's talk about it later."

In the evening, Herb might be tired, and snooze while the news chattered on. If I talked about that idea I had in the morning, some pressing, urgent matter of world importance (in my mind), he might look at me with old eyes and say gently, "Oh, Annie. It's too late in the day to have such a deep discussion. Let's talk about it later."

This is not to say that we did not talk about things of deep importance, but it is a simple description of something I heard from him at times, and with that lesson, I learned that it usually does not take much to really say what needs to be said. Most of what concerned me that seemed of such urgent need to discuss was a deflection of what really needed to be addressed—an emotion, or a need to identify a responsibility, or make a specific request. I learned that the less said, the more is communicated. I learned that a gentle approach with calmness advanced solutions further and quicker than deep, detailed examinations of all the possible angles of an issue. I learned to be attentive, as well as more circumspect in dealing with issues of importance, and to distill down the essentials of what was at the core of my concerns. Now that Herb is gone from my sight, it's harder for me to remember those lessons, but I try to return to them and reflect on them.

This was a good way to proceed through our life together, and saved us many long hours of useless discussion, and helped us avoid contentious disagreements. We were able to solve big problems with simple solutions by attending gently to the essentials and seeking the simple path. I believe this is the lesson we learned in the North Door direction on the Medicine Wheel, the essential knowledge for an Elder to bring forward wisdom in a way which can inspire youth to develop their own vision.

Elders can help reinforce the strength we have gained from our journey and be willing to share with younger people. We can't give up just because we're tired and feel we've already done enough. Maybe that's why so many of the water protectors who are placing their lives on the line today in the face of the onslaught of pipelines are elderly women. They're representing the wisdom of Mother Earth, and we need to listen and truly hear what they are saying. Our survival and the survival of the generations yet to come depends on it.

There were so many teachings from the Elders with whom Herb worked during the years he trained with them. I was never able to meet any of them in person but felt that I "met" them through listening to him teach. The lessons about the "rascals" stayed with me and balanced out the teachings he gave on the Medicine Wheel concepts. Rascals represented the shadow side of the Medicine Wheel illustrating the duality we must face in this life. Things aren't simply "either/or"—they're "both/and."

For Herb, the simple teachings about the "rascals" conveyed all he needed to know about what goes wrong in the world, and what causes individuals and families the most trouble. He believed that, by practicing the traditional Native teachings, one would be able to deal with these five negative issues in life. He held "the rascals" responsible for the environmental damage that has been done to the Earth and its people, and he believed if we worked on dealing appropriately with all that those "rascals" represented, we could help heal Mother Earth. At the same time, he would say, "She doesn't need us to heal Her—She can do that all on her own—She just needs people to stop hurting Her!" He believed there was not much time left to change things and believed that humans were imminently close to facing a worse environmental disaster than had ever happened in human memory. He said his Elders had told him many innocents would suffer at that time, but that Creator "would not allow a hand full of fools to destroy Mother Earth."

Once we went to see a movie that portrayed the history of royal life in England in the 17th century. Leaving the theatre Herb laughingly said, "We just watched a movie about the rascals! Look at all that has happened because of those rascals." I knew what he meant. He was indirectly referring to the legacy of damage done to the world, destroying Indigenous knowledges and spirit around the planet through the destructive conquest of colonialism and capitalism. We spent the rest of the evening discussing with our friends how inferiority, envy, resentment, apathy, and jealousy feed the drives of greed, dominance, fear, rage, and destruction. Herb talked about the role of these "rascals" in his own life and said that it was important to respect them:

> *They have a lot of strength and you need to respect that, take it seriously, and deal with it. Inferiority, if not dealt with in the right way, can lead to domestic violence and destruction when people strike out at those they feel inferior to. Envy is when you*

Enough Light for the Next Step | 119

want something but you don't want to work for it and it can eat you up and destroy you and stop you from being able to work for what you need. Envy disempowers people who give in to it. Resentment means to look over and over at things that have happened and are past. You are re-feeling the feelings of hurt that you received and they fester and hold you back. Not-caring is when you don't help yourself or others; you don't give back to your people or your community. Jealousy wants something you believe you can't have or something you believe others have and you want to take it from them. It is the cause of bitterness and hatred between people. It's a part of domestic violence, too, losing control of yourself and trying to control another.

This is a composite quote, but I've listened to him in various settings speak for hours about the things contained in this one paragraph. He had so many wonderful teachings that he could speak about extemporaneously for days. I once heard him give a four-hour talk on the topic of "The Four Levels of Knowledge Above the Ground." He drew a rough sketch of the concept as represented by the structure of the Sweat Lodge and spoke eloquently and tirelessly about each level. Now I wish I'd been able to record all those teachings, but he rarely recorded his speaking engagements. I would give anything to hear him speak again about the wisdom that he loved so much. The traditional teachings on the sacred concepts were what he loved most in his life. They *were* his life.

CHANGE

THE CALL OF ADVENTURE

"I'm an urban Indian, not a bush Indian," Herb would sometimes say.
Other times, jokingly, he would say, "I'm just an old bush Indian,"
or, "I'm just a Joe Canadian!" There were hidden meanings to these
comments, not all of which were readily understood by people who
heard him say them. At the root of it all was the ambiguous loss of the
childhood spent in nature. The good memories that he had about those
times were a powerful call from nature for him. He enjoyed the quietness
and life of natural settings, like walking in the bush or along the shore of
Lake Superior close to our home. Yet it was very true that Herb did not
like to go camping—I was the person in our partnership who longed for
outdoor experiences of primitive camping and took advantage of every
opportunity to explore a new adventure in the outdoors.

When Herb was a child, whole families traveled together into the
bush to trap, to gather blueberries and cranberries, to fish, and to gather
natural medicines and foods. They traveled to their traditional family
trapping grounds by train, which went through Pic Mobert Reserve,
White River, and east toward Sudbury, taking with them the canoes they
used to travel on the waterways into their family territories. The groups
of people would climb on board the train with all their supplies needed
for the months in the bush and get dropped off beside the railroad line
out in the wilderness, hours away. Boarding several families, the canoes
and equipment, packs of bedding, clothing, food, and supplies, was an
involved process. Things needed to be safely stowed in the baggage car,
and seating found for everyone. It could be a confusing, hectic time.

Herb shared a memory of a time when he was around the age of 5
or 6. It was on one of these adventurous, exciting, and happy trips where
he saw, for the first time in his life, the cruel and frightening violence of
racism directed at his mother. As the family was attempting to climb on
board the train, with young children and babies, bags of belongings and

other items, one of the conductors became impatient and grabbed his mother, cursing at her, calling her a "dirty Indian bitch." He shoved her hard against the steps, causing her to fall. Herb remembered the instant terror he felt, which increased when he saw his father grab the conductor by the neck and hold him up against the train. He heard his father yell at the man, "If I ever see that happen again, I'll fuckin' kill you!" Apparently, other things were also said, a great commotion ensued, but eventually the family was boarded. He remembered that, later on, the conductor came to their seat and apologized, and no one would look at him.

At that age, Herb was still adjusting to having a father. He had been born while his father was away with the Canadian forces during World War II, returning to the Reserve sometime around Herb's 3rd or 4th year. In his child's mind, the unknown mystery of the man who was his father could only be explained by the words, "soldier" and "war." For the child who witnessed his father in a physical altercation with a scary, mean person, this was someone who was a hero, who would set everything right, be strong and powerful, but who was also a bit frightening himself. There were other memories Herb had of his father that were frightening, but for the most part, he always portrayed him as an admirable, strong, and kind man, the hero to the child, yet there were ambivalences as well in his telling of some of the memories he shared with me.

About a year after we met, Herb shared his feelings about having lost the ability to work in nature, losing his arm, and his photographic memory, and how those things were what he missed more than anything else. Given how intelligent he was, how gifted and eloquent, I can only imagine what his life might have been like if the head injury and loss of his arm had not occurred. Herb always said he probably would have ended up driving a truck, but I imagine a life as a doctor or lawyer might have been possible, as his father had dreamed.

Reading was always difficult for Herb after that encounter with the train, and he did not often sit down and read a whole book. He used them as references and resources, dipping into them to learn something he could not learn otherwise. He loved it when I read to him from passages or chapters of the books I was studying, and we could talk for hours about the ideas we were encountering. When we traveled together, I would tell him stories about the things we saw and share what I learned from reading about the places we visited.

On our last journey together, the cruise to the Bahamas, Herb was preoccupied with the physical changes occurring in his body, which neither of us understood, but the highlight of the trip was the afternoon spent with a guide who gave him an oral history of the island we were on, its plants and their medicinal uses, and the story of the nature around us. We later talked about that specific experience in the last weeks of his life. He said he most loved seeing the sharks feeding and learning about the trees and plants.

Herb's adventures took him from coast to coast to coast in Canada and the United States, and to New Zealand, Tahiti, Argentina, Brazil, Ireland, Scotland, and Mexico several times. His last adventure was the cruise, but his declining health meant he stayed in the cabin most of the time, sleeping, and not able to enjoy the views from the deck. He experienced an episode of extremely low blood sugar that landed him in the ship's hospital for an evening, a frightening indication of something seriously going wrong. When we arrived back in Ft. Lauderdale, Florida, he was happy to just stay in the hotel, resting for several days before travelling back home. This was unlike him and was a sure sign all was not as it appeared, and we needed to get home and to his doctor soon.

Despite this difficulty, however, he eagerly set out with me and our friend, Joy, one day for an adventure to visit the Seminole Nation in the Everglades. The hours spent at the museum there, which included a special arrangement to meet with one of the archaeologists, gave him great happiness. The young woman who was our guide was Seminole/ Ojibway and had lived at White Earth, Minnesota, where she learned to speak the Ojibway language. Their conversations in his language delighted Herb. This last trip to Florida and the Bahamas was deeply satisfying to him and seemed to be the final adventure he needed before he could lay down his work and get ready to travel home.

Herb was at peace about his final journey, more so than anyone else around him, but even so, he felt it to be quite a blow that he would not have a last summer at our home together. I will never forget the stricken expression on his face as he sat in his wheelchair in our living room, when he turned to look at me and quietly said, "Hearing it is fourth stage liver cancer was quite a blow."

He had one final naming ceremony to complete and then he was ready, and he set out quite peacefully in his sleep on his final adventure. The young woman whose naming ceremony was completed in the final six hours of Herb's life was my niece. They had spoken together several times about this, and when it was apparent that little time was left, she and her family traveled all night from Oklahoma to our home at Pic River to complete this important task. They arrived just in time for my brother, a nurse, to help Herb transfer from his bed to his wheelchair. He had just awakened from a sleep only to discover that he had suddenly lost the ability to stand. My brother's arrival facilitated a final ceremony that was so important to Herb, and was a priceless gift to my niece, who gave him tobacco and requested a name. The opportunity to sit in final ceremony with Herb and the many family members gathered together was a treasured gift to us all.

Some months after the naming ceremony, my niece wrote to me, and eloquently described her own personal journey with her *Nimishoome*. She spoke of her memories of our wedding, her feelings about the special relationship she felt with Herb, and the impact that the experience of her naming ceremony has had in her life. She felt so profoundly accepted by his loving care in giving her a name, confirming a connection she feels to the natural world. The naming ceremony was a pivotal part of a significant developmental stage in my niece's life. She was on the cusp of becoming the young woman she has grown to be.

The gift to Herb was that doing this special ceremony gave him a tangible, concrete outlet to complete his calling on this Earth. Being able to do this, in a circle of family and friends in the intimacy of his own home, with his Ceremonial Bundle laid out before him on the Turtle Teaching Blanket that meant so much to him, gave him the control of completion, the fulfillment of choice. He was able to lie down in his bed in peace and was serene in the hours of passage. He briefly had a time of agitation, confusion, and insistence that something needed to happen. When he struggled to get out of his hospital bed, he said, "Annie! It's time to sleep! It's time to go to our bed and sleep!" It took some effort on my part, and his daughter's part, to persuade him that he was already in bed and only needed to rest. It was the only struggle I observed in him in the final days. He departed within hours.

Herb's way of looking at life gave him the understanding that he did not really own anything at all, and he would sometimes say, "The spot I happen to be standing on is the place Creator gave me. It is the only thing I own." Thus, he was at home no matter where he went, whether sitting in his office at Laurentian University, or teaching in a windblown field by "standing stones" in Barra, Ireland, or meeting with the Prime Minister and other dignitaries at a university in New Zealand, or working with students in Mexico, Argentina, or Brazil, or sitting by a sacred fire anywhere on Turtle Island. The one thing that never changed for Herb was his sense that his true home was in the Sweat Lodge, conducting ceremony, sharing his teachings, fulfilling the role of Elder that the Creator called him to take.

There were times in our life together when that role was a great burden to him. Sometimes I would see him deep in thought, or zoned out on the couch half asleep, and ask if everything was alright. Most of the times, he would reply, "Of course," and I would know not to ask more about whatever was on his mind. There were other times, though, when he took the opportunity to unburden himself about what was deep in his heart.

At the conclusion of one of these discussions, he told me, "I think it's time for me to let go of the work at the jail. There's just too much darkness there that I can't help, and it opens up that deep, dark hole in me. It's too hard to keep doing that." I was glad to see him begin to let go of the driving desire to do all he could do, all of the time. As he neared his late sixties, I was relieved to see him begin to take things easier, because I had begun to worry about his diabetes, increased sleeping, forgetfulness and word-finding difficulties.

Around this time, he started to need insulin to keep the diabetic symptoms under control. This was one of the hardest challenges he'd had to deal with in a long time. He really did not want to "take the needle" as he called it, seeing it as something of a death sentence. Like so many people, he equated being on insulin as the end of the line for a diabetic, but resisting it was not the answer. So off we went to diabetic classes together, and I learned to help him with testing his blood sugars and doing insulin injections properly, something I would never have imagined being able to do since I had little love for the medical world. I was a social worker, not a nurse. I could listen to someone talk about their medical problems, but I did not want to do hands-on physical care.

We adapted. We changed. We made use of all the tools and helpers we needed to master this new stage, and we shared many chuckles and gave each other plenty of praise for managing the transition as well as we did. Who would have imagined on the day of our wedding that he would allow me to clip his nails, or test his blood, or that I would be able to give an injection? He took responsibility for managing his illness, scheduling the doctor visits, and sorting out his medications. I never worried that things were not being treated appropriately, even though I worried about symptoms triggered by fluctuating blood sugar levels.

The journey with diabetes is one Herb traveled for many decades of his life, like so many other people. Indigenous peoples seem to share a unique vulnerability to this disease, primarily as a result of chronic trauma and stress from the effects of colonization, intergenerational trauma, imposition of Western foods, and being cut off from traditional support systems, spiritual practices, natural healing methods, and lifestyles. Food insecurity brought on by the changes of colonial domination has heavily impacted the health of Indigenous peoples everywhere. As for his own illness, Herb just blamed the diabetes on his drinking history, and his love of snacks.

He did some research around the late 1980s or early 1990s with First Nation people from Manitoulin Island on their journey with diabetes and, some time afterward, was invited to give a presentation to a gathering of Turtle Island Indigenous health leaders being held in Arizona.

When Herb got off the plane in Phoenix, he found a taxi to drive him to the hotel, and with the help of the taxi driver, got his belongings into the car, and off they went. When they arrived at the hotel, as soon as he stepped out of the taxi, he was swarmed by police officers screaming at him with guns drawn to put his hands up. Since he had only one hand, and was terrified and shocked by this rude greeting, he was a bit slow in responding. He was immediately and roughly bundled into a waiting police car and shackled to an officer, since it would be ridiculous to cuff his one and only arm. At the police station as he was being interrogated, he insisted he was a professor from a university in Canada, invited to speak at a conference there in Phoenix, and could they please call someone from the university?

He was not believed. In fact, the officers insisted he was the one-armed bandit who had just escaped from prison, and they had a photo to prove it. They showed him a photo of himself. Actually, it was a photo of another man who resembled him so closely he could immediately understand the mistaken identity. What he could never understand was their reluctance to confirm any of the information he provided, their total discounting of his very Canadian accent, identification documents, and passport, derisively claiming they were counterfeits, and their refusal to call the University.

Eventually, someone relented, the phone call was placed, and the University president himself came to the police station to vouch for him and take him on to safer quarters. Herb never forgot that experience of mistaken identity. It was a more traumatic experience than any of his encounters with police officers during his drinking career, and he was forever sensitized to the plight of minority peoples who encounter profiling and brutality from unethical or poorly trained law enforcement officers. Individual law enforcement people were alright to work with or even befriend, but police forces in general got little deference from Herb. He also vowed to never set foot in Arizona again, and he did not. Even when I suggested that the Grand Canyon might make a great location for a vacation, he wasn't interested if it involved going to Arizona.

I heard him recount this story several times, and never heard it change or be embellished from the version he first shared with me. Once, while cleaning out some of his files at the time of his retirement, we found the letter the university president had written to him, apologizing for his experience and expressing deep mortification that the keynote speaker for their special conference had been treated so deplorably. Herb didn't want to save the letter any longer and threw it in the trash. He said he wasn't interested in dwelling on it—it was history, just one of those things that "happens all the time to Indians." There was bitterness and resignation in that statement, but there was also weary acceptance, an acknowledgement of the realities that Indigenous peoples live with everywhere. Discrimination and misunderstanding, ignorance and mistreatment, and murder are a fact of life for Indigenous peoples, so

Enough Light for the Next Step | 127

much so that there's little to do except the slow, steady work of resistance in rebuilding courage, power and knowledge, and moving toward slow change. This is how Herb moved forward. It's how he strove to let go of helpless, ineffective rage against racism. He could not afford to keep the deep anger he had held in his younger years—his sobriety would be threatened by that. He put his energies into teaching, leading, studying, sharing, living, laughing, and loving.

When he got ill on our last vacation together, it was a rude awakening that a huge change was occurring in this journey with diabetes. There was a new front to battle, and it was very personal. It was now time for me to step in and be a medical advocate for him in order to monitor things in a more direct manner. As it turned out, the diabetes problems that became so evident on that last trip were the result of the cancer that had begun to grow rapidly in his liver. I had to "up my game" very quickly, and we both recognized that things were changing dramatically. It was a shocking, sudden awakening out of a long, pleasant dream into a cold reality—his life was coming to a conclusion, and our life together was undergoing a dramatic disruption.

From the perspective of months and years later, I believe that our life together is continuing, but in a vastly different way than I ever could have imagined. After the death of an intimate companion, everything changes profoundly, especially for the partner left behind. Shortly after Herb's death, I visited my 94-year-old uncle, who had been widowed seven years previously. "Annie," he said, "it's an experience unlike any other experience in life you will ever have!" He was so right, and I was so bewildered.

Over the years, following Herb's death, my personal goal of writing about the things Herb had wanted to put into his second book, which we'd been unable to complete, has been a guiding light for me. It has been a way for me to continue the conversation with him and hold closely the treasure of his wisdom. I can embrace the journey and allow the thread of our spiritual connection to pull me through deep, seemingly endless waters.

Times have changed. Herb no longer walks this Earth or stands in the spot Creator placed him, but he is finally "home," I believe, in a space that is truly his. I own the journey I am still on and accept the tasks ahead of me as my way of "stepping up to the plate" and taking a swing at that ball speeding at me. I can imagine him saying, "You can do it, lovey!" (I sometimes wondered if he called me "lovey" or "chum" because he couldn't remember my name!). As I work on this project and others, I can almost hear him saying one of the last things he said to me, just hours before he died. He reached out and held my arm and said, "Annie, I love you so much!" That memory inspires me and urges me on.

Rascals and Helpers

Every day is a new challenge when one needs to manage with only one arm, as Herb did for the last 53 years of his life. He did it quite well as far as I could observe, but then, I only knew him for the last 10 ½ years of his life. From the stories he shared with me, and what he wrote about in his book, I know quite well the years prior to 1979, when he began the path of healing through his Native traditions, were filled with bitterness and many deep frustrations and angers.

Whenever Herb experienced difficulties with his emotions, he would work on using Medicine Wheel teachings to help himself move toward mastering what troubled him. When he observed in social settings comments or actions that were disturbing, he would say, "There are the rascals," meaning that one of the negative forces was at work. He believed that every conflict within and among human beings could be traced back to the rascals, and to the biggest, most fundamental rascal of all, fear.

I have found it useful in my life to consider these concepts as a way of observing myself and my thoughts and feelings whenever I encounter disturbance in or around me. Often, I am keenly aware the rascals are ruling my thoughts, emotions, and actions. Thinking about this allows me to get some distance from what is happening in my mind and influencing my choices, and it gives me a starting point for knowing how to defuse from the negative attachment and move toward getting a better handle on my emotions. When I'm just not able to do so, it helps me get enough perspective on the problem, the poor actions or judgments on my part, to say, "Well, there are those rascals showing up again."

If, for example, I can identify that my inner imbalance is rooted in fear, I can reflect on the bigger picture beyond my own small viewpoint. I can imagine I'm in the large universe looking at my small self on this tiny planet and see myself as part of something much bigger than myself. I can say, "I see myself feeling the feeling of hurt," or anger or resentment or whatever the problem is. It helps me get perspective. Nothing really is holding me back from looking at fears differently. I can allow that "bigger part" to calm, soothe and comfort the small distress that I am feeling. Reflection can help me act, or take small steps to calm the distress.

In this way, my spirit, or imagination, helps me to accept responsibility for my own feeling as opposed to staying stuck in a victim position. Taking action is important and needs to be done in a good way. My efforts won't always go smoothly or perfectly, but with other people's help, I can stay balanced. There are options for me. I can take action to protect myself, or ask for help from others, or take a break and focus on good self-care, and let go of whatever is out of my control. I can focus on actions to reduce anxiety and let go of distress, even if it takes me some time to get to that point.

The other side of this reflection is the reality that racial, economic, political, and sexual oppression in the larger societal structures around me give power to "rascals" much larger than my small self alone can possibly push back. Multiple aspects of privilege exist in my life, yet there is little I can do about the bigger issues. I have to recognize that billions and billions of humans, and the whole natural world, are negatively impacted by processes of domination and control. It is solely the power of love and relationship which can provide power to effect change in the larger world. My experience with brain injury also informs me that we humans can't always control our immediate, basic biological and neurological responses to our physical circumstances. I must be patient with myself, and with others, and understand that being in touch with the best of my inner self may not always be possible. Balance is not always possible when the pendulum is swinging wildly.

By looking at current crises in this way, I see that I do not need to live in fear or operate my life choices from a defensive position. I can confront problems head on instead of hiding or retreating. I can make a good choice. I can remain open, knowing that I'm part of a larger reality. I'm just one very small person, and I can do only my own small part, but how powerful it is to unhook myself from the striving and struggling to battle whatever it is that I fear and dislike. It's okay to connect with other people and to ask for help. All that from staring the rascal of fear in the eye, respecting its teachings and direction, and picking up my responsibility. Saying this is very easy, but it is something I must continuously work on. I'm very grateful for the patience of people in my life.

Living this way has been a great comfort to me, especially in the time since Herb has walked on "to the other side of the camp," as a friend of ours put it. I feel connected to the comfort his presence brings to my inner world. It connects me to the good things I learned in my Mennonite childhood despite all the struggles I have had with that legacy. The one "leftover" that I have yet to get a good handle on is the rascal of guilt, which goes along with a sense of inferiority. Herb did not have much use for guilt. He didn't talk about that. He saw it as useless, something that was left over from colonization, something that was used, along with fear, against Indigenous peoples to take away their traditions, their land and resources, and their whole way of life. Guilt, shame, and blame are things to let go of by doing the work of being responsible for one's actions, and not blaming an external or internal force separate from the self. "Feeling guilty never changed anyone," he would say. "You have to work on yourself and make those changes and not waste energy on guilt." He really wanted me to get rid of this rascal.

Herb had remarked to me many times that he believed the traditional teachings could restore the identity of Indigenous peoples if only they could learn how to apply them in practical ways in day-to-day life. He said there were so many people who knew intellectually about the traditional teachings but had no clue how to make them work in their lives and relationships. He said so often, "They can't make the journey from the mind to the heart and put it into practical effect."

The practical side of the traditions, as applied to daily life, meant he tried hard to listen, reflect, and work hard on himself, to value and take care of himself, and to care about other people. He wanted so very much to be a good husband, and to be helpful, kind, caring, and giving. "Look for what needs to be done and do it before being asked. My grandfather taught me that," he shared. "It isn't hard to do. It just takes willingness and time and attention." He developed this quality over years of practice and commitment, and it wasn't work, it was love. It also wasn't perfect. There were times when his efforts fell flat, and selfishness showed its trickster nature.

Herb truly believed every person could have a good life, despite all the problems they faced. He believed a peaceful and successful life was possible if traditional teachings were put into action. He had realized in his own life the transformative power of the teachings, and all the warm and wonderful love that had been brought to him over the years as the teachings continued to heal him. He was a work in progress. He was not perfect, nor had he solved all the unresolved issues he carried with him. There was still room for improvement. But he was content, satisfied, assured that he had done his good work to the best of his ability, and when it came time to go, he was ready. He had no regrets.

I began to learn how to apply the traditions and teachings through my experiences of the Sweat Lodge ceremonies that I was welcomed into. That first year of our life together, I went into many of the lodges during the winter. In the deep wintertime of northern Ontario, snow covers everything. The air is crisp with freezing temperatures, and the Northern Lights, sometimes softly glowing in the sky and sometimes undulating in great ribbons high into the night sky, are awe-inspiring to see as they caress the arching sky. On a full-moon night, it's easy to walk under the stars and be able to see clearly—the snow itself seems to glow with a blue-white light. Day or night, the sacred ceremony was always very special—each one different in its own way.

We went to a Sweat Lodge every other weekend in our first winter together. *Shkabeas*—the fire keeper and helper—tended the sacred fire heating the Grandfathers, the rocks that would come into the Sweat Lodge with us and release their healing energies. Standing around the fire, sometimes while it was snowing, before the time was right to start the ceremony, we had time to reflect, pray, and listen to the teachings that Herb or *Shkabeas* would give to prepare for our time in Creator's presence. Going into the Sweat Lodge felt like the safest place in the world to be.

Some of the most profound healings I've received came to me in that first year of our life together as I experienced the routine of praying in the Sweat Lodge and learned the teachings of the Spirit. Grief, sorrow, rage, fear, woundedness, loss, abandonment, inferiority, resentment, guilt—so many of the damaging emotions we struggle with as humans—all poured out of my soul there in the heat of the Womb of Mother Earth. I believe it helped to re-wire my brain in a happier direction.

One dark winter's night, as I breathed in the steam from water sprinkled on the glowing rocks, I relaxed as the sweat poured from my body, absorbed by the deep peace brought by drum songs, the smell of sage smudge and tobacco smoke from the Elder's pipe, and the Medicines of cedar, sweetgrass, and others sprinkled on the Grandfathers. In a deep silence, I saw a form appear. It was the ancient form of a Grandmother Turtle, rising large and silent in front of me from the glowing rocks, looking wordlessly deep into my mind, my heart, my soul. The silence around me intensified, and I felt the timelessness of the universe settling around me as I relaxed into her wise, ancient gaze, so patient, so much love pouring into me. After a long while, she faded into darkness and there was only the heat, and tiny sparkling lights flickering occasionally, and the soft prayers of others in the lodge with me. I remember every sensual aspect of that event and feel the calm settle into me with the memory.

In the months after Herb's death, it was difficult for me to feel calm and at peace. It was hard to remember the Grandmother Turtle. When I really needed to "turtle" and draw into myself for a while, I instead compulsively cleaned and reorganized and set about to change my surroundings. Rooms got painted, closets, drawers, and shelves cleaned, pictures moved, clothing packed.

Eventually, I decided to fly to California and take a long drive back to my home in Canada with a friend. We stopped in Oklahoma at my brother's farm and visited his family's beautiful country setting for a few days. One hot afternoon, I walked alone across a field, down a hill through tall grasses and small trees to an embankment where a meandering stream flowed across sedimentary rocks formed eons ago.

I sat on a rock and watched the cool water flow by, saw the small fossils in the rocks, and glimpsed what seemed to be a small dinosaur skeleton. There were many such fossils on my brother's land, which fascinated and intrigued me. How small and brief our lives seem in contrast to the ancient record of fossils. As I sat there in the hot sun, I saw a tiny green turtle floating down the stream. It stopped right in front of me, clinging to a reed growing at the edge of the water. The turtle seemed to like it there, and I gazed at its tiny form, hanging strongly onto the reed waving back and forth in the flow of water. I became sleepy, laid down on the warm rock, and closed my eyes, drifting off to sleep with the gentle sound of water trickling past. It was so peaceful there, and my sad heart was comforted.

When I woke from my brief nap, the tiny green turtle was still there, seemingly happy with her precarious perch on the waving reed. I wanted to pick her up, but refrained, imagining that a small turtle would be over-stressed if plucked out of its happy place by a mysterious intrusive giant. And then, in a moment, the turtle was gone, down the stream in the flow of water, off to some other perch. I remembered the ancient Grandmother Turtle that had appeared to me in the Sweat Lodge so many years before and thought what a contrast in images this was. At the beginning of my years with Herb, I met the ancient one. At the end of our years together, I met the infant one.

Some of the Turtle teachings I received from Herb came to him from his years spent with the Elders who trained him. The first time I heard him explain the "directions" of the Sweat Lodge, was our first meeting, which took place in the Sweat Lodge. I learned that the entrance to the Lodge was oriented toward the eastern "door" and represented by the Turtle, *Mackinac*. When we were all seated on the ground in the lodge, in a circle around the pit for the Grandfathers (the hot rocks), blankets were drawn across the door opening, and all we could see were the rocks, glowing a deep red in the darkness. Herb gave the teachings of the Turtle, who came to heal the broken hearts and spirits of the people.

There was such tenderness in his voice as he spoke of the ways by which the Spirit of the Turtle works to mend the brokenness of a human heart. Each time I heard Herb speak in the Sweat Lodge about the Turtle, it held a special significance because it represented for me the beginning of something wonderful—a vision of what life could be like with non-judgmental healing replacing religious dogma. Slowly, slowly, over the years the understandings seeped into me, and the multitude of prayers lifted to the Creator as we meditated on the lessons of the Turtle Spirit knit together many of the broken places in my own heart, the heart of a wounded healer.

Herb once told me that the Turtle teaches us caring, service, and generosity. He would sometimes recognize a person's gift as being that of the Turtle Spirit, evidenced by their kindness and helpful nature, and give them a gift to acknowledge that he saw the Turtle Spirit in them.

Not everyone would understand that, but receiving recognition for the gifts that you carry in your relationships is important. Usually, the person receiving that recognition would experience some amazement that Herb could see something in them that they might not have recognized themselves. These kinds of things were important to him, and I believe he thought about them in ways that few could truly understand. He recognized my Turtle Spirit.

My Turtle Spirit moves slowly sometimes, seems to be asleep other times, and there are times a lot of ground is covered quickly. I see things other people miss, hear things others might not hear, and make choices that may seem strange to many. In late 2017, in the small Vermont town where I lived briefly for a time, I stopped by the road to assist a woman standing in the snow and ice, looking around as if lost. Everyone else was zooming past—maybe they didn't see her in the thick, blowing snow, but I saw her out of the corner of my eye, and I knew she needed something. It was almost Christmas, a season when everyone rushes around, too busy to perceive what is reaching out for them. I chose to turn around and stop.

"Do you need some help?" I asked.

She looked at me, smiled, and then looked away. "I think so," she replied. I didn't recognize her accent, perhaps she was from Africa, or somewhere in the south, or perhaps she lived in town, but she was not someone I had seen before, and the three big suitcases covered in snow by her side told their own story, revealing the heavy burdens she was carrying. She was alone. No one was coming to pick her up. She mentioned the library might be a good place to go, and we tossed back and forth some ideas of what might be the best thing to do.

When I found out that she had a cousin who lived in a town about 40 miles away, I said, "That's not too far for me to drive. Shall I take you there?"

"No. She can't get me until tomorrow. I need to stay here and wait for her, but I thought maybe I could find a church, or...." Her voice faded away and she did not look at me again. "She said she could pick me up at the Rodeway Inn."

"That's just up the road," I replied. "I would be glad to drive you there."

Then she looked at me, and a smile lit up the deep hue of her warm face, and her dark eyes, like the Grandmother Turtle's eyes, sparkled. She laughed and said, "But I don't have any money!"

It did not take me long to figure out what was the only acceptable response. "I have just enough left on my credit card to put you up for the night. How about if I take you to the Rodeway and get a room for you? I'm more than glad to do that. It would be my way of paying it forward for all the people who have given me so much help over the years."

I waited while she thought. I remained still, respected her need to have a choice in a hard situation. I knew how to talk just enough to do some problem solving, and how to be quiet and not intrude into a process that was solely hers to navigate. It can be hard to allow people to reach out and help, something I had learned well in the difficult months after my car accident. Eventually, she said, "Thank you, ma'am! Thank you so much! I don't know ..." but then I stopped her and told her it was alright.

"My name is Annie. Please don't call me ma'am. I'm just an Annie!" We struggled together to get all her big suitcases into my little car and drove up the road through the blinding snowstorm, and then fought with the luggage again to get it into the hotel room. Later, I went back with a cash gift from my neighbour, and we went to lunch at the drop-in centre. We sat together at the table in the warm, safe space with delicious smells of lunch wafting from behind a counter. While we ate, we watched snow falling, creating a mystical view of the mountain across the river. Before we left, a worker at the center handed me a big bag of brown rice and a large squash and told us to come back.

"I think I could like it here in this town," she said softly as we left. "Even with the cold, I think I could like it here." I wonder now, did we recognize each other's Turtle spirit?

I left her back at the hotel with my phone number, but she never called, and I hope she's safe wherever she is. She didn't offer any contact information and I didn't ask, but I'll always remember her, the lunch we had together, and the brief conversations. So many people have passed through my life and I've had so many conversations that were completed quickly or left incomplete. I would like a longer, slower conversation, a space where there are fewer goodbyes to be said, but yet, these are the conversations that make up a large part of who I am.

The wisdom of Turtle teaches me much about staying still, being quiet, accepting what is, letting go and moving on in my own way at my own pace. The life I had with Herb is part of that stream of conversations and I learn now to let go, to float on the stream of my life ahead.

Our ten years together went by so fast. Some days I would say, "Sweetheart, it feels like we just got married yesterday, but the way we're together, we could have been married 30 years. It seems like we've been together forever!" I'm not sure what he thought about my expression of feelings on the subject, but I know that the last ten years of his life were some of his best, and mine too, and I know I will treasure our time together forever. We learned much together about the rascals and the helpers.

The simple act of getting up in the morning and preparing for the day taught me that it was much better to do so in a slow and measured, calm and happy way, not the usual rushing around at the last minute after the alarm went off. Sleep was never a good friend of mine, but in the years with Herb, I eventually learned to wake up early, take my time, and have a leisurely breakfast in a peaceful environment before heading out to face the world and the busy tasks of the day. When we lived in Sudbury, Herb would head off to his office at the University and I would either go to the library to study, or simply head to my desk at home.

Herb received many invitations to go to gatherings and give teachings. Sometimes there were day-long workshops, or weekend events, and I was always welcome to go along. I became a helper, a literal "right hand," and easily facilitated processes that had been more difficult for him before I came along—things like smudging, or helping with the Pipe, which went a bit easier with three hands instead of one. So many little things that two-handed people take for granted can make life challenging when one lives with only one arm as Herb had done for so long. He never complained or showed frustration, and never thought of himself as disabled. He was so natural and accepting of having only one arm that often people forgot he was one-armed. I learned to anticipate what little gestures would be helpful, and just went ahead and did them. I learned when not to help, too, and how to not interfere with something he chose to tackle on his own. We worked well together.

Having only one arm created a balance challenge for him. There was nothing to counter-balance the other arm, so I learned to unobtrusively stand beside him in ways that made it easy to quickly steady him so he did not fall over. The year before we met, he had been sitting by a sacred fire and in attempting to get up out of the chair, had toppled over and rolled into the fire, unable to get himself up. Fortunately, others were there to quickly pull him away, and he only had some singed hair and a small burn on his ear. That experience was one he spoke of often to me. As he aged, he became slower and more cautious about his movements. He told me once that I "made a good post" when he was leaning on me as we moved through the darkness from a sweat lodge to the lighted shelter. I think Herb felt more comfortable with having me around so that he did not need to ask other people for help.

Only once did I hear Herb voice frustration about having only one arm. It was an unusually severe snow day in Pic River, with high winds and bitterly cold temperatures of the kind one finds north of Lake Superior in the winter months. I needed to get the driveway cleared so I could head toward my office in town. As I went outside with the shovel he said with a sad look, "This is when I wish I had both arms. I should be the one doing that!" He often started my car so it would be warm for my drive into town, which could take half an hour or more on snow days, and he fought with the scraper and brush to get the ice and snow cleared for me.

I so much appreciated his determined thoughtfulness. One of the teachings Herb gave at presentations was on affection and paying attention. He said, "See what needs to be done, and help before you are asked." These are wonderful things for partners to do for each other. I used to tell him, "I should clone you! You're the best husband in the world!" Some of my friends would say, "Everyone needs a Herb!" as they observed how he was attentive to things that added quality to my life— little, thoughtful things that most would probably not notice, but which made a big difference to me.

One morning, Herb woke with a happy look on his face and told me he had just had a beautiful dream. "I dreamt I was in the bush chopping wood, like in the old days, and I had both arms and it felt so good!" His joy of re-experiencing that physical prowess in his dream was evident in his demeanor. There was no grief or anger about not still having both arms—there was joy that he had once had that experience of working vigorously in the bush and had been able to relive it in a dream.

Herb had a remarkable way of living in the moment. He called it "the eternal now" and he stayed in that present moment all the time. He had little concept of calendar time and could seldom be pinned down to specific time markers when reminiscing about an event. No matter when he was asked, he would say we got married "just about a year or two ago," whether it was five years later or longer.

I loved this aspect of Herb, but it could also be quite confusing at times as I attempted to understand a realistic tracing of his life line—where he had lived during what time period of his life, what he had done, when and where—it was all the same to him, and he truly did not want to be bothered to sort it all out in linear fashion. It took my mind a long time to allow this non-linear "timelessness" to unfold into a different dimensional experience with him.

His ordinary yet very traditional way of telling a story meandered through time and space and unfolded differently than the linear mind formulates sequences, and his way of "filling in the blanks" sometimes led to what could be perceived by others as "fabrication" or "embellishment." I learned that just because something may not be exactly factual, it could still be "true" in a way that represented something with validity. In life, things are not always as they seem, and the apparent reality of a thing may not be its true nature. Storytellers seldom repeat the exact same words when recounting a story, but that does not diminish the true nature, or "truth," of oral history. The telling illustrates an idea with immediate intention, and new and old wisdom is layered through the telling and re-telling, with all its variations, to suit the current, temporal needs for the lesson.

ℒ

Herb loved to go shopping, and whenever he rambled around the mall, which was a favourite hangout of his in whatever city he found himself, he looked for things to buy for me. It was usually something small, maybe something I already had, but his generosity knew no bounds. He could surprise me with a book of poetry or a piece of jewelry, socks or notebooks, a computer, or a crock pot—I never knew what it would be. I had enough toothpaste, shampoo, laundry soap, and paper towels to last a year after he died. It was his great pleasure to always have what was needed on hand.

I heard many stories about his grandparents. It was important for them to have cans of milk on hand during the long winter months, when access to the store could be an endeavor of several days' effort, so his grandfather would stock up whenever he had the chance. Herb said that his maternal grandfather, *Mishomis*, learned how to read English from the printing on the paper wrapper around the can of milk. *Mishomis* was from the James Bay region and knew how to read and write the Cree syllabics, so when he received letters from his sisters up north, he was able to read and catch up on the news from home. Apparently, *Nokomis* liked to tease him about that, saying he was reading letters from his girlfriend. When they married, she was 14 and he was 17, and the day of their wedding was the first time they saw each other. The marriage was arranged by the priest, and she consented because, as she told her grandson, Herb, *Mishomis* "looked pretty good."

Mishomis spoke Cree and *Nokomis* spoke Ojibway, but they understood each other, and they understood English, although they could not speak it fluently. The language Herb learned was an Oji-Cree dialect of the Pic Mobert area, but I was also told that the language spoken in that region was said to be one of the oldest forms of *Anishnaabemowin*. The language used to be a fluid, living form of communication, but after the government effort to "take the Indian out of the child" in residential schools over the course of more than 100 years, and confining Indigenous populations to Reserves, the language has become static and brittle, disconnected from the life-ways of old. It was almost lost completely, but attempts are being made to restore the language and its various dialects, and now there are all the attendant contested understandings of what is the "right way" to say something.

Language is more than a way to communicate. Language is an identity indicator, a way to transmit culture, and First Nation communities struggle to keep their connections to their language. Until Herb went to residential school, he spoke mostly *Anishnaabemowin*, and never had his hair cut. The first day of school was a cruel shock as he was slapped for speaking his own language, the first time in his life he had been treated so harshly. His long braids were cut off, and thus began the education of Herb. He became the man who lost much of his language.

When Herb spoke of his childhood, it was seldom about the hard months at residential school, and more often about the memories he had from his early years. They began to fade in the last few years of his life, and there were things he wanted to remember, but could not. Some things never fade, though, and those are things that affect the heart, positive or negative. Herb chose to focus more on the positive memories as an antidote to the negative ones. He said that dwelling on those negative things would create too many rascals for him, too much anger, and he had learned in his life that he could not afford to let anger take up residence inside of him. That was the worst thing about his drinking days—the deep, deep anger he carried with him then. Walking that "Red Road" for him meant that he focused on managing his negative emotions and staying away from events and relationships that generated a helpless rage response. He had his way of remaining grounded in the traditional healing that restored his identity.

Herb would become very quiet when he was processing difficult memories or thoughts. Once, we drove to White River, about an hour from our home, with his sister, Dorothy, to gather sage. She had heard that good sage was growing near the railroad tracks, so we went in search of the right place. As I remember it, the day was pleasant and warm, and it was an adventure of sorts, but Herb became quieter and quieter as the time of searching for and picking sage stretched into the sunny afternoon.

Dorothy and I were picking sage when I noticed him walking back toward the car, so I followed him and then he told me that this was the first time in over 50 years that he had revisited the site of the horrible train accident that took his arm. I was shocked to learn that we were at the exact spot where the tragedy had unfolded, and turned to ask Dorothy if she had known. "Yes," she said, and then pointed, "And there is the house where I was when I saw the train stopping." Turning, she pointed again, and said, "And there is the path I ran down to find my brother. I just knew somehow that something bad had happened to him." She was 12 years old and was the first person to find him, bleeding, injured, and dying, by the tracks. She ran screaming for help. I was stunned to think that she had not mentioned this before we went to that spot.

Herb did not want to stay there, so I walked back to the car with him.

He told me he felt a bit strange, and we had a few moments to talk about what normally happens when trauma is being processed in the body. He wanted to be distracted from his discomfort, so we started talking about other memories he had of the area, how different things looked now, and where the old field had been, where horses stayed, and the old train station, and other things. We put on some music in the car, and, on the way home, mostly just listened to the music as I drove. After that, I never mentioned the experience again. It was obvious to me that my husband had his own way of dealing with past trauma, a way that did not always include me.

I think, as Herb grew older, some of his life before he met the Elders who worked with him became vague and distant. He once told me he felt as if all that drinking had happened to another person, and that he was not the same man he had been then. It had become like an old nightmare. The traditions that brought his healing and restored his identity were the reality. The Elders were the helpers who introduced him to his traditions and the Creator, and all that had healed him, had restored what was once destroyed by colonization. Practicing the traditions meant it was not always necessary to process things verbally. The wisdom of the ceremonies took care of it all.

I did not grow up with any connections to the traditional life-ways of Herb's people, so I had a lot to learn in our life together. I grew up in a traditional Mennonite community, but my parents, for various reasons and in various ways, were not stereotypical Mennonites. My experiences in the formative years of my early life helped to carve me into a person who lived on the margins between many social realities. I learned to move between my Mennonite life at home and "the world" where I had to go to school. I learned to walk the line between two cultures and survive in both. It was good training for the life I had with Herb, but it left me with a deep ambivalence in my heart. His unconditional love and acceptance helped me to overcome many old wounds.

Early on I had to learn to move between shadow and light, to be present in the storm, and to keep my balance when walking on the knife-edge between fear and longing. That did not always go well for me, or for my parents, and they were little prepared to guide a child who thought differently than they did. My developing brain triggered reactions of temper tantrums when the tension between shadow and light became too overwhelming, and the rage of grief became intolerable. I had great difficulty throughout my life learning to manage strong emotions or contain distress. My mother's response to my distress was to become more punitive, because that was all she had known. My father's response was to become more distant, because that was all he had known—abandonment.

Being introduced to Herb's traditions opened my eyes into another way of perceiving my "rascals" and exercising my "helpers." The boundless curiosity and driving urge to explore that I had had as a child did not fit well with the busy, demanding work of the small medical mission where I lived when very young. Later, in Lancaster, Pennsylvania, the Mennonite environment was a tight knit cocoon separating me from larger realities. Curiosity, however, helped me meet the challenges of moving into adult life, getting higher education, and becoming a clinical social worker. Living with Herb expanded my view in deeper, spiritual ways, and continues to help me open and "ripen."

As an adult, studying to be a therapist, I discovered I needed to follow the trail carved out by my early life experiences and face the inner problems created by the physical, verbal, and emotional abuse I had experienced as a child. The violence was never predictable, and months or even years could go by in relative peace before the unpredictable explosions would occur, or they could happen daily for a period of time—one never knew. The discrepancy of living within a culture and religion that taught peace and non-violence, while at the same time needing to manage the grief and terror of a dysfunctional and abusive environment, led me to dissociate many aspects of myself.

Not knowing what to name my struggles contributed to my inner challenges, but as an adult, finding the name for it—adverse childhood experiences (ACE)—I only felt a greater inner storm. The result of being bullied in public school for being a Mennonite also had a heavy impact on me, as it contributed to living with an inner and outer split. I pretended not to be a Mennonite as much as possible, but shuttling back and forth between two identities caused significant personal damage. Hiding the bigger part of yourself is not a healthy way to live.

I have spent my life on a path of learning from the multiple realities of my world and creating something good out of what was destructive of positive development. To know that my mother's goal was positive, and that she truly did love me, was something I only discovered as an adult, due in part to Herb's help, but it has never been an easy knowledge to completely incorporate into myself. The search for identity is ongoing and follows a unique and interesting path.

When I met Herb, and encountered "the Seven Grandfather Teachings," I found them to be universal wisdom principles that spoke to a deep place within me, helping me to better organize my thinking about my life foundations. They resonated with many of the core positive values I had managed to absorb from my Mennonite heritage and my professional knowledge. The "Grandfather Teachings" are a simple and elegant system to help guide decisions and support positive actions in one's life, and more than anything, they formed the basis of everything Herb held dear to him. He loved and lived the teachings and credited them for saving him from the destruction of addiction.

It's difficult for people like me, for the settler descendants and immigrants who live on this continent, to see our reality through the Indigenous lens. It's necessary to come to terms with what it means to benefit from historical and ongoing cultural and physical genocide of the First Peoples of this continent. Living with Herb and being immersed in Anishnaabeg life for over ten years in his community facilitated my awareness in new dimensions. Within our relationship, we shared our understandings of the realities of our different worlds, and the Teachings were our guide and our place to find common ground on which to stand together. We both grew spiritually, we both experienced healing of deep wounds in simple ways, and we both learned from each other.

Today, I am aware that two of those teachings hold special wisdom for me as I navigate the challenges I face in entering the final stage of my life. I'm stretching myself further to embrace the Indigenous worldview and pushing myself to grow wiser and kinder in the face of greater losses. The two teachings *Zaagidwin* (Love) and *Gwekwaadziwin* (Honesty) hold the secret for me to be able to stand in the face of adversity and conflict. These are my helpers and I use them as well as I can to deal with things that seem to endlessly trip me as I travel on in my life.

We live in a time of chaos that is accelerating in all kinds of ways—

environmental crises, social and economic problems, challenges with technology and internet safety, world-wide political conflict, war, pandemic, massive waves of human migrations, human trafficking, catastrophic extinctions...the list seems endless. It's profoundly overwhelming for most of us. It challenges our sense of what is real and what can be trusted. Humans do not yet know how to remain human in the face of such rapid and overwhelming change. Our brains are about 50,000 years behind our technology. We need to remain calm in the face of the storm, but for too many humans the storm spins life out of control and they begin to flail about, hurting each other *and* their physical and social environments. We can be knocked over by the inner and outer storms. We are like hurting, frightened children.

The skill of facing each other in the storm and not reacting out of fear with efforts to control things requires that we learn to stay in communication lovingly and honestly. While I am bereft of the physical presence of the amazing human being who was my husband, I still have the traditions he shared to help me live lovingly and honestly. I still have my personal core values shaped in my early years with values of compassion and service. I have determination to keep my head up and feed the fire in myself so that I can continue to carry forward good teachings to the best of my ability. Some days, my abilities are on the weaker end of the spectrum, and some days, I am strong. It helps when I am connected with other people who understand traditional teachings.

THE SIMPLE THINGS OF LIFE

A big adjustment I had to make when I moved to Sudbury was to follow a diabetic diet for our meals. I had a tiny bit of knowledge about the importance of this from my experiences with gestational diabetes during both of my pregnancies, but it was a challenge to cook for Herb, whose diabetes was much more severe. Prior to my appearance in his life, he'd been prone to snacking on unhealthy but easy-to-eat foods like chips and pies and ice cream, and his "kitchen" was located in Gloria's Restaurant, where his favorite meal was a big plate of pasta and Marinara sauce, followed by bread pudding for dessert. "Salads are too difficult to chew," he said, which was true due to the dental issues he had struggled with his whole life. His sister used to say if she couldn't find Herb at home, she just called the restaurant and asked for him. It was a friendly place where people knew him on a first-name basis, and he met many friends there. But the food was not necessarily friendly to a diabetic.

My appearance in his life changed all that, and before long he was raving about my cooking and not in such a big hurry to go visit Gloria. I learned why he didn't like cooked carrots (they had been shoved down his throat in residential school) and understood that fresh fruits needed to be sliced into small portions so he could chew them. I learned that he loved fried fish, mustard pickles, and raw onions because they reminded him of favourite foods in childhood, along with cooked white beans, boiled potatoes, and fried sausages. He also loved nothing more than to buy a hot dog fresh from a food stand, loaded with sauerkraut, mustard and ketchup. Of course, the condiments readily made a dressing for his shirt. In fact, I used to tease him that no meal was complete if he wasn't feeding his shirt. He took a lot of teasing from friends over the way food fell out of his mouth as he ate and ended up on his clothing or the floor.

Herb ate with gusto and enjoyed all kinds of food. His all-time favourite, however, hands down, was slow cooked pot roast with moose meat, onions, turnips, and potatoes. Each year, he was the recipient of moose meat from his friend and colleague Vince Pawis, who harvested moose for the Elders in the traditional way. Herb felt content and happy when the new supply of moose meat was safely stowed away in our little freezer. It was with great pleasure and satisfaction that we ate our share over the winter months. I made moose meat sausages and baked them with tomato sauce, cooked moose stews in the pressure cooker so that the meat was tender enough to melt in the mouth, and invited family and friends to share moose roasts with us many winter evenings.

The heart of what food meant to Herb was good feelings. This fit with teachings he had about the East Door of the Medicine Wheel, the direction of vision, good food, balanced emotions, and the experiences of childhood. He could talk for hours about the teachings of the East Door and how significant they were in establishing a good life—*minobimaadiziwin*. Taking care of one's body and eating good food was the key to being healthy, as well as having good eyesight and a vision for one's life. He knew well the consequences of not respecting the teachings of this direction from the years of alcoholism that had ravaged his body. The cirrhosis scarring, which he was not aware of, eventually prevented the treatment of the liver cancer that took his life. He commented once that he knew why his grandfather lived so long—because he'd eaten good food from the bush and hadn't spent years drinking alcohol.

. In the later years of his life with me, he became willing to take to heart the things he learned from nurses and healers who urged him to eliminate certain foods from his diet. Bacon, chips, candy, and pie disappeared from his list. Pork in general was a rarity. He'd been told by another Elder that pork meat didn't digest well, due to its similarity to human flesh. Nonetheless, he loved to order pork chops occasionally when eating out in a restaurant, with pudding for dessert.

Usually Herb tried to avoid the "Five White Gifts from the White Man"—white sugar, white flour, white potatoes, white rice, and white bread. Eventually, bread and processed cereals went the way of potato chips, but his cooked oats and Red River Cereal remained a favourite breakfast food. Nothing made Herb happier than to have me cook porridge with raisins for him in the morning. Battered fried fish gave way to baked or poached fish, skim milk took the place of whole milk, and berry smoothies turned out to be a good substitute for ice cream and pudding, as well as being a great bedtime snack. Still, doughnuts, pies, and chips were treasured treats to be consumed on rare occasions—or when

I was out of town. Our sister-in-law, Sheila, tells with lots of laughter, the time she and his brother, Don, came home to find a bag of snacks hanging on their doorknob. "Annie must be coming home," she said to Don.

One of the last meals I wanted to cook for Herb was one of his favourites—white fish poached in coconut milk with leeks and kale—but his appetite was gone, and within days, his body was gone, too. The fish remained in the freezer a long time before I could bear to cook it and eat it alone. Not being able to cook for Herb anymore was a surprising loss for me, and I still miss that caring act.

Repetition of healthy patterns is an important element of a stable life, and Herb and I were able to maintain these patterns of healthy repetition in our life together. Sometimes, we would go over memories together that we had talked about before, or reminiscence about trips we had taken together, visits we'd had with family and friends. Always, when Herb was talking about the traditional teachings, there was repetition. He told the same story over and over, but there were slight variations depending on the setting of the event. The way he shared those teachings in his classroom at Laurentian University was different than how it would be re-told at a ceremony for young people out in the bush.

One of the things I remember most about Herb's friend John was his statement, "Herb tells the same story every time." He was referring to the teachings Herb always gave at the beginning of a Sweat Lodge Ceremony. When traditional Elders share a teaching, the task of the listener is to absorb it in all of its spiritual dimensions. Because it is a spiritual story, the variation is always there, layered in ever deepening levels of meaning. Thus, the listeners know that Spirit is alive, constantly working to shape the story to the present context, containing the wisdom of the past, which is so integral for the journey into the future. Spirit is never static, nor is culture. The culture may change, the language by which the story is transmitted may change, but the truth in the spiritual story remains constantly alive, dynamic, in flux yet never changing in truth or intention. Story carries its own wisdom, and knowledge its own Spirit.

The traditional wisdom transmitted to Herb through repetition over the years he worked with his Elders added to the ancient truths he had absorbed in the years of his childhood in the bush. So much had been lost through colonization and the oppression of the Church and the destruction of the old ways, yet essential knowledge was carried on. Many stories and teachings remained hidden because the older people would not speak about them openly due to their fear of what would happen if the authorities discovered they were practicing the old ways. The children knew the old ones had hidden knowledge. They wanted to know the secrets of their elders. Herb's generation went seeking for those old stories, that ancient wisdom. Fortunately, there were people still alive in his time who had received the ancient wisdom passed down to them, and they could teach and share the deep traditions. His Elders carried knowledge from time immemorial, and gave it to Herb to pass on, and he passed it on to so many people.

In his book, *The Hollow Tree: Fighting Addiction with Traditional Native Healing* (2006), Herb wrote eloquently about his experiences in regaining his traditions and the restorative power they held for him. He always acknowledged his teachers when he shared his stories, and also the Creator's gift to him in allowing him to find his truth. It was a path he knew he would only complete when he went to the Creator's home. He wholly accepted where he was on his own journey, and also accepted others wherever they were on their journey. If they didn't want to listen, it just meant they were not ready. He truly tried hard to be patient and non-judgmental, yet he was firm about the truth he carried.

Herb had little time or patience for those who sought to impose their own rigidity on these teachings. He did not argue with them, but usually accepted that they were on their own learning curve. He went his own way and allowed others to go theirs. In the face of ignorance, apathy, or strong opposing opinions, he was more likely to become silent than to argue, but sometimes, he would rebuke a way of thinking or acting if he felt it was interfering with the work of the Spirit. If someone's behaviour was interfering with other people in a ceremony, he would directly address the situation, sometimes to their displeasure or embarrassment, but he also readily welcomed sincere amends and efforts to restore harmony and balance. Even in conflict situations at the University, he generally displayed these characteristics, although he could also be confrontational in reaction to racist statements. Herb had no time for people who clung to ignorance.

Mostly, Herb became a channel for the Spirit to take care of things and he was confident that the Creator "would not allow a handful of fools" to ruin things irreparably, either in a ceremony or on the planet. He knew he wasn't perfect and accepted that he would make mistakes but trusted that Creator knew his intentions were good and that Creator would help him. He universally accepted that a larger force than himself was at work, and never took credit for the remarkable things that sometimes occurred in his ceremonies. The credit went to the Creator. If disrespectful people were making fun of the stories, he would give them a choice to stay and participate respectfully or remove themselves. He knew that if they would stay and accept the experience for what it was for them, they would have a remarkable spiritual encounter.

I heard him share a story about some teenagers who had been acting out and how the Spirit intervened in the mystical form of an Eagle in the Sweat Lodge and spoke into the ear of each of the young people. They were from the city with backgrounds from many different First Nations, and none could speak their own Indigenous languages. He saw the Eagle Spirit speak to them audibly, to each in their own language, and they understood what was said and compared notes amongst each other later. All had received the same message, and all of the teens experienced a remarkable and dramatic change in their demeanor and behaviour for the rest of the camping weekend.

These types of things were not unexpected in Herb's Sweat Lodge ceremonies, but also not every ceremony was as dramatic as that. He always said it was not up to him, but up to the Creator as to what would happen. He could not make something happen or not happen. He was only the facilitator, not the controller. Physical and emotional healings sometimes happened in the Sweat Lodge with amazing changes coming into people's lives afterwards.

The Sweat Lodge Ceremony was not the one most commonly conducted by Herb. More often, he held a traditional Pipe Ceremony and Talking Circle where the Eagle Feather was passed, and each person had the opportunity to hold it as they spoke their truth, or simply passed it on to the next person. Herb started off the Talking Circle by, again, repeating a story, the same old story each time, but with a different slant to meet the needs of the situation in front of him.

When introducing traditional concepts to a group of people who had never encountered an *Anishnaabeg* Elder before, he was patient and open, reassuring and gentle. Most non-Indigenous people have no concept of their role as immigrants, settler descendants and Treaty People with responsibilities. Their ignorance handicaps them and impairs their ability to relate to Indigenous peoples appropriately. They can sometimes feel intimidated around Indigenous peoples and not know what to do or say. Sometimes, they're fearful of "making mistakes." Sometimes, they are arrogant and insulting even without intending to be so, and sometimes, they intend to assert their perceived dominance.

Herb's teachings had a great impact on the non-Indigenous peoples he worked with. He showed them love. He had a deep desire to see change happen for the Indigenous peoples of the world and his prayer was always that he would be able, in his own small way, to carry some truth to them that would bring about healing. He was open to non-Indigenous peoples, maybe more so than many traditional teachers, because he believed that change had to happen from both directions. The non-Indigenous peoples needed healing as much as the Indigenous peoples.

Herb was one of those rare, authentic people for whom there were no strangers, only friends he did not yet know. He had a special gift for being able to read people, and he knew when someone was not sincere. He respected "real" people and avoided the others. If someone greatly offended him, or misused him, he would never associate with them again, but he also would not go out of his way to speak ill of them. He never sought revenge. Rarely, he would confront them strongly and immediately, but he extended forgiveness readily if the offending individual was sincere in making amends. If they continued in their racist or ignorant stance, he would have nothing further to do with them and would not go to great lengths to seek reconciliation. He believed they had the right to walk their own path, and it was Creator's job, not his, to change them.

People who were "real" could listen to Herb tell the old stories over and over again, and never tire of the repetition. Every telling held a truth for them when they listened in the right way, with openness and no judgment. Herb generously shared his gifts, doing only what was asked and not "marketing" himself or pushing himself in where he was not welcome. His humble leadership touched the lives of countless people around the world as he shared his knowledge, the same story, but new each time it was told. His friend, Charlene, a non-Indigenous woman whose life work has been to serve Indigenous children and families, wrote to me after his death to share her story. Her letter illustrates so much of who he was, and what I want to share about him.

> Herb was . . . the most sincere, honest and gentle man I have ever known. He was my teacher, my friend and my chum. I first met Herb in 1988 before Native Child and Family Services [in Toronto] opened its doors for operation. I had arrived from British Columbia a year previously and was looking for an opportunity to work in the community again after working in Bella Bella and with the Nuu-Cha-Nulth Tribal Council.

> Herb was to interview me for a frontline Social Work position. I was very eager and scared, expecting a formal interview. It was far from it. Herb interviewed me at Fran's Restaurant on the corner of College and Yonge. He immediately set me to ease with his humour and gentleness. The interview lasted for almost two hours and by the end he knew my whole life story. He was interested in me as a Human Being and took time to develop trust and to start what was to be a long-lasting relationship that spanned many years.

> Herb was the Elder of Native Child as well as our supervisor. To start the agency off in a good way Herb suggested all staff including the receptionist embark on a four day fast without food and water. We were to be together as a united group to vision for the agency and to set things in motion. I was petrified to say the least but Herb in his gentleness let all the female staff pitch tents close together for support.
> The fast was the beginning of his many teachings and ceremonies. I must admit I cannot remember a lot of those four days. I remember my eyes sunk in and I used my cotton sheet

as Kleenex for the allergies I developed. I remember meeting Alana his daughter who was 13 years old at the time and how impressed I was with her wisdom at such a young age. I also remember breaking the fast with water and realizing how precious that first sip was. I remember a group of 7 or 8 individuals walking into a Chinese Restaurant in Buckhorn, dirty, disheveled, and a little out of it. I remember all of us women heading straight for the washroom to try and clean up. I remember how nonchalant Herb was about the whole thing. What a sight we must have been but Herb did not worry about such things. He was not one for pompous ceremony or for making a social impression. He was genuine through and through.

The first year of operation Herb and I continued to develop our relationship. One day as I was on the streetcar rushing to get to work because I was late, I bumped into Herb. As we got off the streetcar Herb waved at me as we passed Fran's and said, "I will see you later, I am going for breakfast." I was surprised to say the least but would learn over the years that Herb had his own relaxed rhythm unlike anyone else.

That first year Herb often conducted talking circles with cloth based on the colours of the Medicine Wheel. He explained that his teachings were from Peter Ocheese and Cree Elders who first introduced Herb to many teachings. He used the Cree Medicine Wheel as the basis of his teachings in a very simple but profound way. Over the years he conducted Sweat Lodge Ceremonies for staff at Curve Lake with Doug Williams. Here too, the teachings of the Medicine Wheel came to life in a profound way.

When Herb left the agency a year later to take a position as a Professor in Sudbury at Laurentian University, I was very sad because I thought I would not see him again. So many people go to new jobs and the relationship ends. Not ours. In fact, once he left the city he began to visit and stay with my family when in town. He loved to talk to my husband about music and we discovered that before his accident he had played the saxophone.

His visits to our home became a regular thing and he often spent Christmas with us and our children over the years. I remember one year, I believe it was 1998, Herb joined my husband and I late at night for four evenings in a row, after the kids were in bed, watching two full series of the Sopranos. He loved to just hang out and go with the flow.

When my teenage daughter brought some friends home one day, he gave them all teachings and presented sweet grass to one of the young men. He told him to use it wisely and if he was going to the bar to put it in his pocket. I was so taken aback with his generosity and non-judgmental manner. The youth loved him and it gave me comfort to remember this exchange because a few months later the young man died in a car crash. Herb held Pipe Ceremonies at my house for family, neighbours, friends of friends, whoever requested it. He always taught me, however, that he would never conduct a ceremony or give a formal teaching unless asked. He did not push anything on anyone and was very respectful of other people's paths and ways.

Herb shared a lot about his life with me. He was particularly close to his Grandmother who taught him that the sun shone for all people regardless of their colour, that there was no colour in the Spirit world and that everyone was welcome. This fundamental teaching made him an Elder for so many. Whenever he conducted a Sweat or had a gathering for teachings it was always attended by people of every race. He did not discriminate or withhold his knowledge and wisdom. He shared it openly and with love. At his 65th Birthday party held on Doug Williams' land there were people from all over the world paying tribute to him. He was humble and gracious as people gathered and gifted him with many presents.

Herb was a man of his word and often went out of his way to help others. He supported me when my sister was diagnosed with a terminal illness. He contacted one of his Healers north of Sudbury, picked my sister and I up, drove many miles with us and introduced my sister to the Healer who worked on her and prepared special medicine. I believe her twenty years of life after that is the result of his medicine and Herb's generosity.

When my granddaughter was born in 2000 Herb agreed to conduct a naming ceremony for her. The name she received was from her Great Aunt in Bella Bella and despite many attempts at correct pronunciation he could not get the Heiltsuk dialect and she was named Honolulu. We all still chuckle over this to this day.

One year our team decided to have a special ceremony for boys 10-12. Herb graciously agreed to put them out to fast for one day on land near his home in Sudbury. Myself and two other staff, with ten very rowdy boys converged on Herb's apartment to spend the night. I never saw Herb get upset or raise his voice but the boys were too much for him and when he bellowed out a very strong "Stop your fighting" the boys stopped and listened. At the fast Herb gave the boys very important teachings about the Fire within and he was gentle and patient with them. All ten boys completed their fast as a result and drove home beaming and proud of their accomplishment.

Over the years I attended numerous sweats and fasts with Herb. One sweat that particularly stands out for me is a sweat the Mooka'am Team and I attended in Sudbury during the dead of winter. Herb arranged for us to be brought to the sweat through the farmers' fields by horses and sled. It was a cold, clear night, the moon was full and shining, the snow crackled under the hooves of the horses and we city folk were mesmerized. We changed by a campfire and crawled and slipped into the sweat over snow and ice to find Herb sitting in the western doorway chuckling at our clumsiness. He lit his pipe and called in the Spirits, instructed the helpers to place his pipe outside the Sweat Lodge behind him. This was to ensure any negativity he picked up would be channeled into the pipe and not stay in his body.

Each summer Herb would drive to Native Child's Camp to provide teachings for children and youth. One summer in 2010, Herb conducted a sweat for a group of teenagers who were doing a cultural exchange with Native Child and the Scarborough Boys and Girls Club. Many of these youths were just being introduced to the teachings and ceremonies and as teenagers were quite rowdy, disrespectful and unresponsive. In Herb's mesmerizing way he was able to harness their excessive energy and had them calm and open to the teachings in less than ten minutes. He invited them to take part either in the Lodge or outside and you know what? The majority came in. His Sweat was gentle yet very profound for them. Most noted this as their highlight of the trip.

I loved seeing Herb at Grundy Lake because he would often whisk me away at the pretense of consulting about an issue and we would disappear to the store down the road for a huge ice cream and some quiet moments to talk about life. We were like two big kids enjoying our melting ice cream, laughing about life and simply enjoying one another's company. He really was my chum.

Over the years we had many intimate talks about life, death, love, and commitment. He would tell me about his experiences and his relationships. He really wanted to commit but was very hesitant and scared. He had very special relationships over the years but he would always tell after they were over that he needed to do his own work and he wasn't sure another marriage was in the cards for him. He praised his ex-wife Sheila who he still had a deep and enduring relationship with and questioned whether he was marriage material. Surprise, surprise, low and behold on one of his trips to the States where he often taught, he met Annie. He told me about her immediately and it was an honour to attend their marriage a year later. His beloved sister Dorothy helped organize the whole affair where many family and friends gathered to experience three days of ceremony. True to Herb's way of life the festivities commenced only after a commitment Sweat on the day before the wedding vows were exchanged. It was a wonderful wedding, filled with laughter and many tears. I remembered sobbing out of both happiness and yes, fear. I thought I had lost one of my best friends. Herb proved me wrong. I became friends with Annie as well.

The last time Herb stayed with me was in 2015 when he attended NCFST's Cultural Retreat to teach and conduct a sweat. He had all kinds of medication as his diabetes had progressed but he was organized and able to provide instructions on how to assist him. We talked until late into the night but he made sure to call Annie and check in. He talked about how proud he was of her, his children, and grandchildren. He had numerous plans for the coming years and was excited to talk about all he wanted to do. When my husband dropped him off at the bus terminal he said, "You know what Art, Charlene is my best friend." When I heard that I cried.

So, as I sit writing this, I know Herb is still around even though he has passed into the spirit world. He continues to play tricks, like deleting two paragraphs I just wrote because he wants us to know there is no end to any of this. It keeps going and going. Love has no boundaries and we all need to put our collective thoughts together to create change and secure the planet for those yet to come.
His teachings live in all who knew him and will continue to carry on through all of us collectively.

Charlene Avalos

The journey from woundedness and despair to living in the light of healing took Herb the larger part of his life to traverse. By the time he was 39 years old, it was clear he would not live very long if he kept doing what he was doing, and only through the Creator's true miracle of purification and restoration was he able to go on to the life he needed. Before embracing this journey, he disdained the "tree huggers" and "Hollywood Indians," and was too filled with bitterness to understand the Indigenous connection to spirit and nature that he had experienced in childhood. He was angry all the time, and especially at white people. As he said one time, "I did not know what my name, *Mahng-ese*, meant." It took him a long time to understand all the meaning carried in his Spirit name, the name his *Nokomis* gave him.

Herb was fortunate enough in childhood to have had a father who spent time with him and talked to him about things of importance, such as the teachings of the Loon Clan, which was the patrilineal clan of his ancestors. Countless times, I heard Herb repeat the story of the time he sat with his father outside their cabin and watching a priest walk by. His family respected that priest, yet his father told him in no uncertain terms not to follow him. He said, "The Loon takes care of the family, and finds food for them. The Loon will never harm the young or rape the children, or misuse or abuse anyone. Don't follow the priest, he will lead you astray."

Herb often used this teaching in his talks with people as it made quite an impression on him as a young boy. He had seen the parent loons with their young, how attached the family groups were and how loyal. His identification with the Loon Clan was restored to him in the years after beginning work with his Elders. He respected the Clan teachings and always sought to learn more. He began to understand the people he used to refer to as "tree huggers." He deepened his feelings about nature and developed a longing to see the Earth be healed from the ravages of modern civilization.

Herb hated to see what was happening with all the environmental destruction on the planet, the poisoning of the water and air, the destruction the mines left in their wake, often with water being irreparably contaminated even deeper into the water table. He often wondered what was going to happen in the generations to come.

From September 2013 to September 2015, Herb served on the Band Council at Pic River First Nation where we had lived since early 2012. He was so happy that his community had asked him to serve in this way and was eager to work with them on issues related to self-governance and the territorial claim they had been working on for many decades. He also served on the Board of the local hospital in Marathon, Ontario and was instrumental in bringing about improved relationships between the hospital and the local Indigenous peoples it served. He was much loved by the Board members and the local physicians and enjoyed being able to develop positive relationships with them.

He also was a favourite guest speaker in the local high school and served as the elder for the First Annual Student Pow Wow at the Marathon High School. The thread that ran through all of this was his desire to heal relationships, heal the land, live in right relationship with Mother Earth, and do his small part, however imperfect that may be. He loved every opportunity he had to teach young people, to take them out into the bush and share his knowledge about the traditional wisdom.

In February 2015, he was asked to speak at a conference at Trent University in Peterborough, Ontario on the topic of Indigenous Knowledge. As he prepared to travel there from our home, which usually took 14 hours by car, he asked me to sit with him and type while he verbalized what he wanted to share. I was not able to attend, but these are the thoughts he shared in preparation:

Indigenous Knowledge grew from thousands of years of research in the natural world and is the foundation of deep respect for all forms of life. The knowledge grew from the territory itself, as did language, and the people lived in a context of relationships and responsibilities with all the natural world, the Creator, and Invisible helpers. Indigenous Knowledge teaches that each aspect of nature creates a circle of relationships, and is the guide to all human choices, and holds the key to understanding.

Language defines our relationships to the land and to each other, and to Shkagamik-Kwe (Mother Earth). Language informs our spiritual understanding and the traditional structure of community. Debwewin (truth) instructs our own personal truths. Our language provides the context for the traditional teachings passed on by our Elders, commonly referred to as oral teachings. This paradigm has been utilized by the Aboriginal community for millennia. Passions in our communities run very deeply when it comes to oral tradition and Indigenous Knowledge.

Medicine Wheel teachings represent Indigenous Knowledge from deep history. The four colors are outlined through the four directions of the Medicine Wheel. The four colors reflect the colors of humanity—red, yellow, black, and white— we are all the same but we are all different, too. Sometimes through that idea of being different conflict emerges between the different peoples. The Elders always pray for peace between and among the four colors that they will be able to control their Five Rascals, inferiority, envy, resentment, not-caring, and jealousy. The Elders seek a journey of peace by lighting the Sacred Fire within the heart of humanity. The heart of humanity is represented on the Medicine Wheel by the color green in the centre. Other colors also have Sacred Teachings. Humanity has traveled through different eras of time. The transition from one time to the next time era is a long struggle. We are now in a time of moving from the Industrial Age to the Age of Information and beyond to the Age of Re-Greening of the Earth. The present desire is for humanity to learn to reduce the use of fossil fuels and nuclear fuels, which create massive destruction to Mother Earth. In the Age of Re-Greening of the Earth the vision would be to heal the Earth from all the damage her little children have created.

Indigenous Knowledge can help us learn how to heal humanity and the Earth. The tens of thousands of years of accumulated wisdom from the Elders and the Ancestors call us to reactivate the circle of relationships in the natural world and among all people. This will take time and effort by each soul; however, the Five Rascals prevent us from doing what is necessary. Indigenous Knowledge can help guide us to a place of healing, learning, growing, and relating in a better way to Mother Earth and among us all.

Even though we have lost many Indigenous languages we still have the Indigenous Knowledge through the teachings of Elders, and in our own blood memory. We still have the capacity to behave as humans and be responsible in our relationships. Indigenous Knowledge is our guide, as are the

Invisible Helpers, the Creator, and the natural world. It is all part of the circle.

It all came down to what he called "the fire within." He spoke about caring for the "fire" in our heart, and how we were connected with the fire at the centre of the Earth and the fire in the sun. The three working together meant all was in balance. Not many people could readily understand the metaphor he was speaking about, and like many Elders, Herb was not quick to explain the metaphor. It was important for people to do the internal, spiritual work of figuring out what their inner fire was all about, and what they needed to do to keep it alive, healthy, and in balance with the other fires. He would speak of "The Three Fires," and to him, it meant being in balance with Earth, self, and Creator. He understood that few people in today's world would do that internal reflective work of trying to understand themselves and work in "right relationship" with nature and with all of creation.

Herb occasionally spoke with me about what his Elders had shared with him about their understanding of the distant future for this Earth. He understood that their teachings were wisdom that came from the Creator, and he recognized it as truth for him. He believed that humans stood at a crossroads, and that it was unknown yet what path they would take—whether to walk a path of respect for all the sacredness of Mother Earth or continue on a path of destruction. He said, "If things go too far, it will be too late for us as humans, but Mother Earth will recover from us. Creator will not let a handful of fools destroy the Earth. She will get along fine without us, but in the meantime, many innocent people will suffer greatly." To damage Mother Earth was a profane act in his eyes.

He believed the crisis time was not far in coming and sometimes was deeply sad about that. He desired so much for more people to understand the sacredness of the Earth, the traditional Indigenous teachings, and their own lives. While he enjoyed nice things, he saw it as foolish to strive to possess more and more material goods at the expense of the Earth. He saw it as the height of hypocrisy for people to talk about the Teachings as if they owned them yet engage in wasteful behaviour that damaged the Earth. He knew his own life was not as consistent with the teachings as he wanted it to be, and he never stopped trying to make things better.

Herb truly understood the link between all of life and how sacred it was, and our responsibilities for how we lived our lives. He was happiest when outside in the bush, by a fire, or walking on the beach by Lake Superior listening to the waves and the sounds of birds. It brought great peace inside himself to be able to connect with Mother Earth.

The year after we moved to Pic River First Nation, the *Idle No More* movement was in full swing in Canada and generated much energy in the country around the issues of reconciliation between non-Indigenous peoples of the country and Indigenous peoples. Actions of resistance of many sorts played out across the country. The little town of Marathon, Ontario, near the Reserve where we lived, sponsored a rally in support of *Idle No More*. Herb and I attended the event, and although he did not speak at it, he later wrote a note for the Pic River community newsletter about his understanding of how the Seven Grandfather teachings integrate with the movement.

The Seven Grandfather Teachings
and the
Idle No More Movement

First, we will list the Seven Grandfather Teachings:

1. Wisdom – to cherish your knowledge

2. Love – to know love is to know peace

3. Bravery – to face your foe with integrity

4. Honesty – to understand honesty is to be authentic and real

5. Humility – is to know yourself as a sacred part of Creation

and Creator; we are all equal, no better or worse than any other part of Creation

6. Respect – "re" means again, and "spect" means to look; we look twice at everything to gain understanding

7. Truth – is to know all of the teachings and apply them in your life; there is only one "truth" which is yours and yours alone, but to understand truth is to know and recognize the truth of others .

The Idle No More movement began in the heart of community life and was started by four women, but it has no official leaders. It has a wide base of support among Native peoples, and non-Native peoples have joined with their support, even around the world.

Basically, Indigenous peoples around the world, like here in Canada, are seeking justice for the Earth and for their communities. There is a strong emphasis on respecting the environment, the life of Indigenous communities, and respecting Treaty agreements going back hundreds of years. More specifically, it seeks to reset our relationship with the Federal government. This reset means honoring the Treaties and the sacredness of life.

The wisdom of the Idle No More movement is based in the love of the Creator and the Earth. It asks the people to bravely face their foe with integrity and non-violence. Like Chief Therese Spence modeling her love and her insistence for fairness and principles, people are asked to sacrifice with honesty and humility, with respect and truth, and to seek right relationships with each other and in all their actions.

Following the Seven Grandfather Teachings, or the Seven Wisdom Teachings as some say, will help us each to know what right action can be taken to support Idle No More. It will be different for different people, and it must remain peaceful in order to find its greatest effectiveness. When we meet resistance from those who are misinformed or lack understanding and respect, we can rely on these traditional teachings to guide our appropriate responses in peaceful ways. We use bravery to speak our truth, and help others step aside from their fear. Frightened people who lack knowledge can act in threatening ways, but if we face them with the traditional teachings, we can deflect their negativity and continue to move forward in a good way.

Teachings about the colours were important to Herb. He loved talking about the things he knew were symbolized by the different colours represented on the Medicine Wheel. His favourite colour was green, which was in the centre of the Medicine Wheel as he knew it. Money was "green power," too, but the other green power that Herb mentioned, at least to me, was the "green power" of Mother Earth. For him, the colour green was the symbol of the great power of the Mother Earth, her love for all of life and the sustenance that was given through her gifts of green plants, green trees, the food, the air, the water, and all the living creatures. When he went to New Zealand, the impression that stayed with him the most was how green everything was in that country, and he spoke fondly of his time spent there, wishing he would have a chance to go back again someday.

On the last night of his life, Herb was awake often. I went to take a little nap, thinking I would wake up in the morning to greet him with a kiss as usual, a hug and a cheerful, "Hi lovey!" which was our favourite greeting in the morning. Herb's daughter, Alana, planned to spend the night on a mattress on the floor by her father's hospital bed in the room which had served as his office. She was up a lot, helping him be more comfortable, or just talking a bit with him when he was awake.

At one point, Alana noticed that her father was looking at the large world map on the wall above his bed and they talked about the different countries he had visited in the last ten years. She asked him which was his favourite country, and after a while he said, "New Zealand." She asked him why that place was so special for him and his reply was, "Green. Green like Mother Earth." Not long after that, Herb fell into a sleep from which he never woke.

It has always seemed significant to me that Herb's final thoughts were about the colour of Mother Earth and the beauty of the planet. He loved the Earth and grieved that humans had brought so much damage and destruction to this precious planet. He believed that if humans could just follow the teachings of the Medicine Wheel, and the sacred teachings of Indigenous Peoples, or even just follow the teachings of the Bible or other sacred scriptures, the Earth might have a chance to heal.

He had wanted us to write a book about his thoughts on the changing world and what was needed to restore respect and right relationship with the environment. He deeply believed people could change because he had changed so much in his own life.

The teachings of the East Door of the Medicine Wheel tell us that, without vision, the people will perish. They will feel inferior and resort to self-destruction and destructive ways of behaving. People who feel inferior will be fearful and attempt to control others and events around them as a way of abdicating their responsibility to seek their own vision and live their own unique life. When Herb was giving a teaching about the East Door, he would say, "You are unique. There is no one like you in the world anywhere and never has been and never will be. You can only be yourself, not anyone else. You can only live your own life." He would draw a comparison with the trees in the forest. "Look at the birch tree. It is not like the spruce, or the cedar, or any other tree. Each birch tree grows in its own way. It's not like any other birch in the forest, even though it is a birch tree and there are many birch trees in the forest."

Stories from nature were woven into Herb's teachings on many things. In so many ways, he felt divided from nature, unable to fully engage in the natural activities he had grown up with because of the loss of his arm. Due to that, he believed he had become "an urban Indian," more comfortable in the city than in the bush. Despite that, he only came fully alive when he was out on the land, by a lake or river, sitting by a campfire, or taking a short walk in a natural setting. It opened up his heart in a way that an excursion to the mall could never do, although that, too, was a favourite past-time for him. He loved to people-watch at the mall or sit with a cup of tea or coffee at a cafe. He felt happy to be around people, and to be around nature. Life was boring to him without those two things.

Restoring the natural connection between people and nature was something Herb recognized as an essential pathway to restoring the Earth from the ravages of industrialization and development. Yet he also recognized that humans today depended on the benefits of what modernization had brought. He once asked someone who was espousing a complete return to the old Native ways, "Do you think you'd be able to live without modern medicine to keep you alive, or without a car to get you around? How do you propose doing without all these things?" The person he was talking with did not have an answer for him.

Another time, someone was criticizing wind turbines and protesting their placement on Manitoulin Island. Herb was upset by that and said, "The colonizers put electric lines here and you benefit from that, and how much does that electricity from coal plants damage the Earth you say you love so much? Why is damaging the Earth so important to you that you don't want better technology which doesn't damage the Earth so much?" Again, there was no answer to that.

He knew about the tar sands in northern Alberta and was opposed to the proposal of a new pipeline going through or near the Pic River First Nation reserve, but it did not stop him from driving his car or taking plane flights when he traveled a far distance. Yet he always was interested in learning about ideas for reducing reliance on fossil fuels and fascinated by science that informed him of the problems and potential solutions. He always wanted to learn.

Herb recognized the monumental task of restoring a better relationship to the Earth, but he also found it deeply troubling that political leaders and a significant portion of the population had no will to do even small things to change and make a difference. He supported people's efforts to live life in a way that was less damaging to the environment, such as recycling. We bought water bottles with filters in them so that we could carry water with us when traveling and not buy water in little plastic bottles. Yet at the same time, if there was a feast or ceremony and water bottles were distributed, he did not criticize.

Herb knew that people were usually doing the best they could with what they had, and that things could not be done a perfect way all the time. He understood the connection between time and relationship, and knew that change takes time, and that working on things over a long time would bring about positive changes. He knew that many different types of people and ways of life were necessary to build a good world and bring about healing. What troubled him were the people who were unwilling to listen, unwilling to invest time into their relationships, and unwilling to learn how to sacrifice to make necessary changes.

His work with people who were fasting usually involved teachings about sacrifice, and he spoke about the tradition of sacrificing the intake of food and water for a period of time as a method of increasing one's ability to hear the Creator. This was necessary in order to learn the small changes they needed to make in order to grow stronger and make the necessary bigger changes in their life. Herb had no illusions that making the changes to save the environment would be an easy, straightforward thing. He knew that people would struggle, and fail, but he believed that the Creator called us to struggle and fail as a way of learning about humility and bravery, and about trusting the Creator to help us change for the sake of Mother Earth.

TRUSTING THE PATH

When I married Herb, I had little trust in most of my relationships, except for a few family members and close friends. My philosophy was, "I trust you if I can see you." While I made my choice to be with Herb based on my assessment that he was a good man, and most likely a highly trustworthy man, there was a deep place inside of me where I harboured a belief that things could change anytime for the worse, and I would not be surprised if they did. Betrayal trauma has real and lasting effects.

It was about a full three years before I realized that this mistrust of my partner was gone, and I no longer harboured doubt in his loyalty to me, or in the viability of our future together. As my trust in our relationship grew, our closeness deepened, and our level of comfort together increased. I relaxed and felt freer in our life together. Things just got easier, and I found myself wondering why things had been so hard in my other relationships? What was the missing element?

It's often said, as if universally true, that good relationships take work. I'm not so sure I believe that, at least in the sense we often have of "work," as if it is a painful struggle and something we would rather avoid. I believe that good relationships require a lot of things, but truly good relationships that work are not "work"—they are fun, fulfilling, generative, satisfying, secure, solid, and trustworthy. They require only a few fundamental things: absolute loyalty and honesty, respect, effort, and unconditional love. That's not "work" — it's a natural connection and needs to be mutual. It cannot be one-sided. If it is one-sided, it can turn into addiction, or dependency and enmeshment, or any other version of a toxic connection. Relationships that are "hot" and conflicted are not truly viable, although they may be exciting, even romantic, or long-lasting. A viable, healthy relationship cannot be based on a trauma bond, which in general means that the attachment between people—parent/child, partner/partner—is locked into an endless cycle of "honeymoon," tension, explosion, remorse and "making up." A healthy, successful relationship is one where both partners grow and are supportive of each other's vital growth. Calm, secure attachment is required for a viable relationship, one that does not become stagnant and die, but transforms daily. The ingredient of a healthy relationship calls for maturity and commitment on the part of both people in the partnership. It is mutual and balanced, not enmeshed with dependency or power and control.

There are a number of requirements for healthy connections to unfold: communication, humility, reliability, emotional regulation and distress tolerance, and the ability to "hang onto the self" and stay grounded no matter what is happening around you. These are the qualities and skills that do require individual work at all stages of life. We are not born automatically having all these skills. We learn them, and earn them, through a lifetime of practice. An unwavering commitment to the self, to the other, and to the "us" has to be present in mature relationships. There is no room for power and control behaviors, selfish attitudes, or thoughtlessness. Without loving characteristics, a relationship is bound to fail under the weight of responsibilities, which only increases as we age. Perhaps these mature qualities and abilities only become strong later in life as one develops wisdom, patience, and tolerance with self and others, or perhaps these are things which can only emerge within nurturing relationships with unquestioned emotional bonds, rooted in something greater than themselves. An example would be the healthy parent-child bond. These are the things that make it possible for deep trust to unfold. There is no such thing as a successful "fast-food" approach to relationships.

Maybe that is part of what is troublesome in the social fabric today— there is so little support for us in safe and nurturing spaces. Too much competition, striving, comparing, needing, and wanting is being acted out in all our relationships, from kindergarten to the boardrooms and government halls. Too much of our relating is transactional rather than mutually relational, respectful, and reciprocal. Too much energy goes into acquiring things, doing rather than being, achieving rather than enjoying, or mediating connections through devices rather than through eye-to-eye connection. Patience, time, and unselfish commitment are required to build trust.

To be free in a relationship means to have freedom to become intimate, not freedom to be detached, distant, and self-preoccupied. People who are motivated to gain only one's own pleasure and satisfaction will lose the opportunity to experience desire in the true give and take of a deep intimacy. They lose an opportunity to experience an honest expression of healthy sexuality. Although Herb and I were both well acquainted with problematic relationships in our younger years, we enjoyed the freedom of true intimacy in our relationship, which was healing for both of us. We were older when we married, needing to deal with common physical problems encountered as people age, but that did not interfere with our closeness and commitment to each other. We neither needed nor wanted anything from the other beyond love, honesty, loyalty, commitment, and safety. We did not demand or expect particular behaviours from each other because we unconditionally loved and accepted the other in all of our splendor and imperfections. We were fortunate to have a high level of compatibility.

Herb and I felt free to be ourselves, at ease, with comfort and relaxation, because there were no comparisons, competitions, or expectations. It was not work, but that does not mean we put no thought or effort into our relating—we did. We were careful, not careless with each other's hearts. We paid attention. We gave each other our time. We did not interfere with each other or our relationship by indulging in addictions, obsessions, or selfish preoccupations. Our communication was clear and open. We didn't close ourselves off from the other, yet we also respected each other's need for time to "recharge" with cherished periods of solitude.

Neither of us wanted to change the other—we just wanted to love and be loved, accept and be accepted. We trusted each other with the gift of our whole Self, and we each respected that gift, were polite, and gentle, and open to having fun with each other. Not a day passed where we didn't share a laugh, a hug, or a kind word or touch. Not to say that there were no irritations—there were, rarely—but we did not express our irritations with anger or hang on to resentment. We spoke our truth with honesty and respect, calmly and assertively, and sought to set things right if hurt had come to the other. We enjoyed comfortable silences and companionable times of simply being together, each doing our own thing. We carried our own responsibility, both of us. No one had to carry more of the emotional responsibility than the other. Every day was a new day with no debts carried over from the day before.

I had not experienced this in any of my previous relationships. I had not seen this kind of easy, loving relationship in my family of origin, or between my parents. It was so liberating to live this way with a true partner, a way I had always believed was possible and had always hoped for, but never fully believed could happen for me. I grew to understand that one of the reasons this was possible for the two of us was because we were each spiritually grounded and could share our spiritual path with each other. We could accept each other's differences and appreciate each other's uniqueness.

Herb had spiritual practices that were rooted in his traditional teachings, one of which was to shake his sacred ceremonial rattle early in the morning to call in the Spirit to be with him. Spirit was being invited into his day, and he was placing himself solidly in the centre of Creator's care for him. "First things first" was a slogan that meant something very real to him, and I respected that. We both had a prayer life, and there were special times when we shared our prayers by smudging and praying together when Herb smoked his pipe, or when we used my pipe that he had gifted me. It was, in part, this prayer life, this spiritual connection, which fed our marriage and made things work effortlessly. Other people have other ways to achieve this level of connectedness, but this is what worked for us. It was the basis of our trust.

I've learned through all of my life experiences to trust that each decision I make to respond to what I sense around me has been part of the gift that Creator has given me. My doubts are part of that trust, which may sound paradoxical, but the truest truths are paradoxes—two opposites both exactly true at the same time. As a child, I was amazed to learn that ice, water, and steam were all forms of H_2O. How could a solid be a liquid, be a vapour, and all be the same thing? That was the beginning of mystery for me, pondering ideas great philosophers have spent lifetimes investigating. I have come to believe that the dreams and visions inside of me are generated by a mutually recursive and generative process of greater consciousness, and both my physical being and conscious reality is a part of that mystery. The two are part of the same thing and go together. I act and respond, and this is part of being guided, protected, gifted, and provided for.

Sometimes, I struggle and lack patience with myself and my world, but I have learned to trust that the Universe is a benevolent reality and love will prevail. Sometimes, I have to talk it through with a trusted friend and voice my doubts and anxieties, my complaints and fears. It's my way of "turning it over" to my Higher Consciousness. I continue each day to learn to trust and make requests, and the answers flow from the universe in ways that reveal truths that have been there all along. Many times, the answers I need emerge as I move forward in trust. I choose to believe the best possible outcome will happen eventually, despite whatever human negativity I may carry, or even in the face of contradictions. Sometimes a thing will not appear to be working out well, but "things are not always as they seem." I strive to accept things as they are, name them for what I think they are, and then simply let them be.

I am part of a larger Wholeness, and Herb was part of that too. He nurtured that in me, and our life together continues to nurture that in me, helping to create a full life without him, yet always with him in a certain sense. I trust the nurturance that this sense of presence brings to my life, and this trust eases the painful loss of our physical life together on this Earth. Neither of us were perfect people, and I don't have a perfect life today—there are losses and griefs, failures and flaws, missed opportunities, unfulfilled dreams and wishes—but I trust that everything is exactly as it needs to be for me to learn the things I need to learn. How could it be otherwise?

Everything in my life today is the result of every choice I, and everyone else who has ever lived, has made. Nothing could be different in this moment. The next moment flows from my choices, and the choices of others. I cannot change the choices of the past, which always live with me in a future ever-present. But the present is always changing and nothing stays the same. Still, the old saying bears repeating, "Things are not always as they seem." Security really is an illusion. I have what I am aware of in any given moment. Reality is not necessarily what I feel, or even what I believe. My perception of reality is pliable, and what is truly real may be hidden from me. What I know solidly is that in my life I have loved and been loved, I trusted and was trusted. I have experienced pain in relationships, disappointment in myself, and all the normal range of human feelings and experiences. I grow with every experience into a greater mystery than my words can express.

There is a gift of trust that I learned in my life with Herb. I can't speak for him, but I know he trusted me, too, and felt my love, and knew we were safe together. Nothing changes this; it just goes on ripening and deepening in my heart as I choose each day to continue to love and trust Creator's guidance and protection, no matter what comes my way. I have survived many very difficult things, and all these things have helped me to grow wiser and better, so I pray for that to continue as long as my life is useful here. Choosing to share my story is my gift to myself, to Herb, to Creator, to everyone. I experience this as all part of something bigger and better than I can fully comprehend. This is a knowledge born from experience. It is not just an intellectual or emotional belief in something external, but is rooted in relationship.

The time in my life of living "after Herb" has only been a few years, yet it hardly seems like more than a breath. In this length of time, I have learned how to breathe again, how to walk while holding my tears, how to nourish myself and live my own solitary life. I have discovered that healing comes in the solitude—and I love that, because, in those times of emptiness, I feel close to the spirit of the man who was so precious to so many, and especially to me. He continues to teach me how to love again, and how to love all that is

Now is the time when I turn toward rebuilding a new life for myself, starting new adventures in new places, and reconnecting with old friends and family. Although sometimes I still think that I shall never again feel *exactly* as happy as I felt with Herb in our years together, I wait patiently for new kinds of joy. I feel grateful for that, too. I think we shared a rare gem of a special relationship that most people don't get to experience; but perhaps others who are bereft of a mate think that as well.

We had 10 years together. In my judgement, that was not enough time for me and our families to share a walk with Herb, but time is immaterial in these matters. I'm sure if it had been 30 years, or 60 years, or longer, we would still feel the same way. I'm happy for him that he has been able to go home to his ultimate healing, to wake up in his heart's home with Creator. He often spoke of being invited into the Creator's home after life on this Earth was over. He said that the Creator would ask for your name and ask you what you wanted. You would then say your Spirit Name and tell Creator you wanted to come into his home. "Sometimes," he said, "Creator will ask you to wait, and clean you with burning cedar smudge, and ask you to think about what you have done during your time on Earth."

Herb strongly believed that everyone would eventually find their place in the Creator's home. A friend of his once asked how much cedar would have to be burned to cleanse "really evil people?" Herb said, "It might take a couple of truck loads, or maybe a whole forest, I don't know, but I believe each of us will find his place in the Creator's own time."

When we are stuck in a blame and shame mentality, it is tempting to fantasize about punishing evil, but that is not where Herb lived. He lived in a transformative mindset, where forgiveness and acceptance were the path to freedom from evil. He could express anger about injustices, and strong opinions about the right ways to live, and still promote the high path to truth and reconciliation. He called himself to a higher standard, even when at times he did not want to. Forgiving the injustices of the Residential School experiences, the genocide and colonization that had robbed the Earth and Indigenous peoples of so much, was a very difficult thing with which he sometimes struggled. He was on a learning curve in his life until the final moments.

The year after Herb's death was very hard for me as I strove to return to a semblance of a normal life and meet my obligations. I was not angry about his death; I accepted it completely, but I had lost our life together, which I treasured, and I feared losing myself also. To distract myself, I traveled a lot, returned to work, and made plans to move from the house we had built. I didn't believe at any point in that year that I could ever get over the feelings of grief, but I had an important event to prepare for which kept me focused—the First Year Anniversary Give-Away Ceremony, the traditional ceremony held to commemorate the life of one who has passed on, when all their possessions are given away. This is a day for the final "letting go." On the day after the Give-Away, I woke to a new feeling. In my journal entry that next morning, I wrote:

The bitterness is gone from the grief. It is cleaner, not so heavy, and I can truly feel that Herb wants me to live and laugh and move on with my life, make myself happy, live how I choose to live and where I choose to live. I am free to go on. This is a gift, to wake with a lighter heart as a result of yesterday's ceremony. I am ready now to move on, free to return for visits, free to make my own choices...I am so grateful for today, for yesterday, for tomorrow. I can smile and laugh again and breathe more lightly.

I went on to write a longer passage in my journal a few days later:

It is now several days past the Sunday of March 12, 2017, where we celebrated the full year after Herb's passing with the Traditional Give-Away Ceremony. Before Herb and I married he asked me to promise that if he died first I would conduct things in a sacred way, take his ashes to the trap line to put them where his ancestors had trapped their furs and lived their lives, and hold a give-away ceremony to distribute all his possessions in a sacred way, and have things conducted properly as the old ones would have done it. This was important to him, and it was part of the agreement we made with each other before we married. He did not want anything done to interfere with the spiritual work that he believed needed to be done—no alcohol or drugs, no greedy hanging onto things, no wallowing in negative emotions. He wanted me to promise him I would honor him in the Old Way. We occasionally talked about it but I did not overly think about the process until reality set in.

The last few months I have been anxious and preoccupied with concerns related to how this would go, feeling that there was a great weight of responsibility on my shoulders for it all, and feeling very alone with it. The encouragement from his cousin Roderick and Don's wife, Sheila, were helpful, and I trusted that all would be done well by the Elder, Robin Cavanaugh. I was relieved by knowing his old friends, Vince and Leo, would be there to help with the Pipe Ceremony, and I had support and help from Lina and Irene, his cousins. Other relatives gave expressions of support as they were able, but the weight of it all often kept me awake at night.

For a year the collection of his things had gradually grown and taken up the majority of space in our utility room, and by the time I had collected other purchased and donated items, a large pile was growing, filling the dining room as well. I am glad I had this year to gather all these things, to make sure that all his items were separated from my own, and now I am free to move on, knowing that I am not taking anything that should not be taken, and confident that everything distributed has gone where it needed to go. Robin brought the sacred bundle which Doug Williams had safeguarded for the year, and carefully went through it with the family, and cleaned the pipes and feathers and smudged everything. It was so comforting to have him here and to know that all was being carried out in accordance with Herb's desires and wishes, and that we were leaving nothing undone.

Months before this event was to take place, I was concerned about the feast food, wishing to find fish to serve at the feast because Herb liked pickerel so much. I asked many people about where to find it, to no avail. Then Lina told me she would try to find some, and she did! On her trip back from Toronto as she sat in the Thunder Bay airport waiting for her luggage, she met a man who was the son of an old friend. He was from Rocky Bay Reserve and he told her he would get her the fish. On a Thursday night after work a few weeks before the Give-Away event, Lina and I drove to Nipigon and waited to meet him at the gas station on the Lake Helen Reserve. When he arrived, we were so surprised to discover that it was not just a large package of fish, but a full container of frozen whole pickerel freshly caught the day before in the lake beneath the ice in nets, done the old traditional way. Two strong men lifted the huge container into my trunk, completely filling it, and it still amazes me that at the end of the two-hour drive home, when we arrived at Lina's house after 10:30 at night, I was able, with the help of Roderick and Lina's granddaughter, to get the container out of the trunk and into her kitchen without losing any fish, fingers, or toes!

The two days following, Lina had the fish thawing in her bathtub, and with the help of her brother and nephew, cleaned and fileted the beautiful pickerel, and on Sunday morning with Charlene Avalos's help, she transformed the fish into beautiful pieces of fried feast food of the kind Herb would have consumed with gusto!

On the drive back from Nipigon that starry night, Lina and I watched the occasional snow flurries, saw northern lights (wawatay) dancing, and talked together about the awesomeness of the gifts coming to Herb's giveaway. Mr. Morriseau, who caught the fish, had not accepted any money, just an offering of a package of tobacco, and lots of shared laughter. It was in keeping with the spirit of the simple man Herb was, a man who trusted implicitly in the Creator's generosity and abundance. He never worried about where things would come from when it was needed, but always trusted so firmly that what was meant to be would be. I hope to learn to relax into that level of acceptance someday, and the memory of that night and the gift of the fish will go a long way toward helping build my trust and confidence so that I can relax without anxiety about anything.

The day before the Give-Away Ceremony we gathered throughout the day in our home to talk over how these things would be conducted, and what were important things to remember. Robin was so helpful as he calmly and gently shared with us his knowledge and understanding of what the teachings were, and how we needed to let go of things in a good way. He was so comforting, with his calmness and humor, as well as his deep emotions. This was a big step for him to take as Herb's student, friend, companion and helper. I was so glad he was there to provide the guidance and leadership that brought us peace of mind and heart.

By the end of the day we had shared stories, food, laughter, and tears, and were ready to talk together as we went through Herb's sacred bundle and discussed what was there and who these items needed to go to and how they were to be cared for. The completion that this process brought to parts of the grief we all carried was remarkable.

On the day of the ceremony we started to gather at the community hall in the late morning and spent several hours arranging everything. Chairs were placed into a circle; tables lined the walls and were filled with items to give to whoever would attend. There was so much—enough for everyone to take plenty for themselves, their family members and friends, and what was left over was taken to the resale shop in Marathon where their sale would support the food pantry. The only forgotten item was a magnetic nametag from his Laurentian days, found on the floor as we cleaned up the next day, and we gave it to his grandson, Kadin.

People started to gather around 12:30 p.m. The pipe carriers arranged their bundles in front of their chairs, people looked at the things filling the tables, and Roderick attended the sacred fire outside which was started with the help of all the Medicines left in Herb's Sacred Bundle. Tobacco ties were distributed, people signed the guest book, and gradually seats filled and then the ceremony began. Robin explained how things would go, the pipe carriers offered tobacco to each other, the drummers sang songs, and while things did not proceed exactly as Robin had planned, it flowed in a seamless and elegant way throughout the afternoon.

Once the pipes and songs were completed, Robin spoke for a while, explaining why we do these ceremonies, and what it all means, sharing the ancient teachings as they have been carried down for thousands of years, protected and carried through the long centuries of oppression when the ceremonies had to go underground. We were reminded that as recently as within Herb's lifetime, in his childhood, these ceremonies were forbidden and the government authorities could come in and stop the proceedings and confiscate all the items, sacred and otherwise, and imprison people for conducting an "illegal" activity. The sadness of that knowledge was overcome by the joy of knowing those days are over and the people and their ways are being restored.

Robin passed the Talking Feather and explained that everyone there who wished to would have an opportunity to share a story or a memory of something from Herb's life that was important, and when we were finished the give-away would begin. We sat and listened patiently for almost 3 hours as many people spoke eloquently or simply about their memories of the remarkable person we were honoring as we said our last goodbyes. I spoke about how I had not wanted to ever say goodbye to him, how he and I had never had that final conversation and said a goodbye to each other, never talked together about the parting we both knew we were facing. I wept as I finally faced his Sacred Bundle and said, "Goodbye, Herb." The sun was shining through the windows high on the walls of the community hall, illuminating so beautifully all the items I had memories of helping Herb use so many times. I had become his right hand and he had come to rely on me as he conducted his ceremonies, just as much as he had relied on other people to do something for him, especially to clean his pipe. Never again will I be able to clean his pipe for him, or clean the eagle fan he used, or hand him his rattle in the sweat lodge. Now there are only memories to treasure. It is finished. This, too, is like a death, and like a birth.

The traditional teachings tell us that in the first year after someone's death, the person's spirit remains in a spiritual level that is very close to us, and that the person's spirit stays close to us to help us and bring some comfort to us. The person who has died needs to move on, to go to other spiritual levels, because they have other work that needs to be done. We need to do our work of letting them go, of acknowledging that we are releasing them to travel and do the work their spirit must do. Without this release they might stay too close to us and thus be unable to complete their journey. There is a continuing relationship with the person who passes over to the other side, but after the first year we must not expect them to stay too close to us.

This is a hard teaching for me, but I recognize it as truth, because it reflects what I saw in my vision dream at the end of my third fast, and what I heard from my own ancestors then about the work that they needed to do on the other side. Without me doing my own work here they would be unable to do the work that was theirs to do on the other side. There is an important connection. It is this understanding that allows me to safely and gently let go of this time in my life that I shared with my husband. I have learned so much, and it is mine to share, and I will continue to learn from his teachings and my experiences. I honor both of us and the memory of our life together by doing things in the sacred way that was so integral to his life, and to the life we shared. It is okay for me to move on, to allow the past to integrate into what will be in my future, but also to let go and not grasp selfishly to a grief that keeps me tied to the past. This letting go process is surprising to me and is his final gift to me, helping me to live again without his physical presence or that close spiritual presence I felt over the past year. There is now a lightness and an openness that brings relief and my burden of grief begins to lessen.

After the sharing was complete, Robin suggested we have the feast because it was already 4 p.m. and people were getting hungry and restless and some needed to leave to travel. The feast had much more food than could possibly be consumed, so the remains also became part of what was given away, and that, too, was a marvelous gift of generosity. So much good came out of this sacred time. So many people, even those not present, were blessed by the day. The give-away process actually was fun and went quickly, and people seemed happy to receive the abundance. I felt so happy that things had gone well and flowed smoothly and everything had worked out. It was such a relief to have all the help and to know that everything had been done in a good way and gone well.

The people who attended the ceremony were not just from the community—many had come from a distance. There were relatives from Long Lac, friends from Fort Francis, Sudbury, Toronto, and other places. Roy Thomas's widow, Louise, owner of the Anishinabe Art Gallery, came from Thunder Bay and shared her story of how Herb had been crucial to the gifts she had received in her life by meeting her husband. She wept as she described how Herb's journey to restoring his soul and his life after healing from his addictions through the traditional ways was pivotal to Roy finding sobriety and saving his own life, going on to meet her and have a family with her.

Herb's daughter, Alana, and son-in-law, Bentley, and his first wife, Sheila, all shared with tears the special memories they held of their experiences with Herb and his remarkable impact on their lives which continues to extend into the generation of his grandchildren. His son and daughter knew him in ways that no others could know him and he holds a unique place in their hearts that no others can really fathom. The loss they feel at his absence is keen and deep, yet they shared generously with the people who had traveled far to be present, both at his funeral and at this give-away, and gave gifts of money to defray the costs of travel.

Herb's sister, Dorothy, and her husband Duncan, spoke about the special relationship they had shared throughout their lives. His brother Don, and wife, also named Sheila, and family members who traveled from Long-Lac, all shared their love and respect for this man. Herb is sorely missed by his family. Mary Elder shared how Herb had welcomed her into ceremonies and given her a name and taught her the traditions, and how he and I had become her family through the open friendship he offered. Charlene Avalos shared the story of how he hired her in the early days, over 30 years ago, at Native Child and Family Services in Toronto, and how he had established the traditional foundations of the agency, which continue to this day. Allen Brand and Jim Rollo shared the stories of how they met Herb, and how he welcomed them into the ceremonies and taught them the Anishnaabeg spiritual ways that had helped them so much for so many decades. The pipe carriers and many other people shared their stories of work he had done with them, at the university, or in other countries around the world, and how far his book had traveled.

Herb's influence has been strong and steady in large and small ways, and continues today to bring forward powerful spiritual messages, open to all people everywhere. He touched so many people around the world and continues on. We all feel the responsibility to continue to carry forward what he taught, and the important messages he gave. He especially loved Mother Earth, and his last evening alive was filled with references to the beautiful world we live in. His last words, spoken to his daughter less than an hour before he breathed his last breath, were, "Green, like Mother Earth."

The legacy that he left calls us to honor the traditions that are Earth based, and to follow the natural laws that sustain life. His passion for the health of the Earth inspires us to work hard to try to heal the wounds of the Earth, and to restore health to the environment, to the human family and the social networks that are embedded in natural ways. This is the legacy he left, which we strive to honor and carry forward, and always remember and work hard to keep alive.

That next morning, for the first time in a year, I woke with the feeling that things could possibly get better. I had been telling myself that things would never get better, but would just eventually be different. I felt that this grief from my husband's death would always grind away at me and keep pain alive in me. I did not understand I needed to complete the conversation. Having had time to ponder on what that conversation needed to be, the gift I am left with is to know that things *will* get better, not just different.

Now, having traveled a distance of thousands of miles and years of hours, I find that the work I have been doing is creating a strong new beginning for me, sufficient to sustain me for whatever time I have left on this Earth. I have work to do, dreams to fulfill, relationships to nurture, things to learn and do, and places to go.

Off to another adventure, with Herb by my side. Not Herb the man, but his memory, his spirit, the memory of our life together. What has passed is not lost, but has become a shining path, like *Gishgaatig*, the Tree of Light, brightening the way as I journey into the marvelous mystery ahead. There is always enough light for the next step. It's a good way to walk.

GLOSSARY

Anishnaabe; Anishnaabeg – The People; plural; – Ojibwa/Ojibway
Anishnaabe-kwe – (Ojibway) woman
Anishnaabemowin – the language spoken by the *Anishnaabeg*
Bihboon – seasons
Baa maa pii; Baa maa; Giwaabamin, baa maa pii minwa – in general, means "goodbye"
Danguay – sister-in-law
Dodem – clan; the animal for the clan
Gishgaatig – the Tree of Light
Gizhaagien – I love you
Gwekwaadziwin – honesty
Gzhiminadoo; Gzhemidoo – (G'Chi-Manitou; Creator; God)
He/She – No *Anishnaabemowin* words delineate gender ("She/He") so Herb would often use these gender words interchangeably, even in the same sentence, to indicate "that one."
Kekionga – central meeting place of the Miami peoples; located at the confluence of the St. Joseph, St. Mary's, and Maumee Rivers in the region of modern-day Fort Wayne, Indiana.
Kewadinong – North wind
Maahng – loon
Midewiwin – Anishnaabeg spiritual society
Minobimaadiziwin – living the good life
Mishomis – grandfather
Nehganawaynamic – under the protection of
Niitaawis – brother-in-law
Nishmaabeg – plural; another way to say (Ojibway) people
Nimishoome – uncle
Nodin – wind
Nokomis – grandmother
Shkabeas – helper
Wawatay – northern lights
Zaagidwin – love

END NOTES

1. Herb's teachings vary slightly from the Ojibway origin stories, etc., found in the works of Basil Johnson, Eddie Benton Banai, Jim Dumont, and others. He was always clear in stating that his teachings came from the Cree Elders he worked with in Western Canada. One of those Elders, who did not want to be named, was a man whose family originally came from Northern Ontario. Herb identified as Oji-Cree since his maternal grandfather was Cree from the James Bay area who travelled down to LongLac, Ontario, in the early 20th Century, and further down to the Pic Mobert area. Herb was not trained in the *Midewiwin* ways of the Ojibway. Although he respected their teachings and ceremonies, he did not feel called to enter into the strict 'Mide' training. His concern was that this form of spiritual training might reflect a fundamentalist mindset that seemed too religious or 'Catholic' to him. It contrasted with the gentle spirituality he experienced and modeled based on what he had received from his Elders. Herb could conduct a ceremony completely in *Anishnaabemowin* if asked to do so, but he always taught that the Creator made all the languages and could understand prayers in any language, even sign language. The words in the glossary above are the words I learned from Herb as he spoke in his own dialect, and may not reflect the spellings or meanings in other forms of *Anishnaabemowin*.

2. P. 27. Nabigon, H., and Wenger-Nabigon, A. (2012). Wise practices in holistic healing and the traditions: An integration of different theoretical approaches. *Native Social Work Journal, 8, Spring 2012.* http://142.51.24.159/dspace/handle/10219/387

3. P. 64. "The Teachings of the Stones," https://youtu.be/vgEoLxOCcUc. YouTube video of Herb in Ireland.

Acknowledgements

Writing, for me, feels solitary and difficult. At the same time, it is deeply satisfying. It's something I do with the love, support, encouragement, and prodding, of many, many people.

I honor and thank the "collective" which is part of the creation of this book. Heather Campbell sparked my commitment to writing, and if not for her patience and belief in me, I could not have persevered. During the year that I lived in Bellows Falls, Vermont after leaving *Biigtigong Nishnaabeg,* I was fortunate to find a writing group and a memoir writing class across the Connecticut River in New Hampshire. My companions were a pure gift from the universe!

My family by marriage, and my birth family and ancestors, my friends and colleagues (many who sent letters to me about their experiences with Herb), Herb's family, friends and ancestors, all the old and new acquaintances who swirl through my life, all the ones who helped with the writing and editing—all helped in the challenge along the way. *Chi-Miigwetch!*

The full picture of all I have to thank and acknowledge extends into all time and all dimensions of existence. I walked alone much of the time, listening to the wind, the water, the birds and animals and trees—especially the cedar trees. Sitting by the water as often as I could, reflecting on thoughts and feelings, listening to the sounds around me, I extended my understanding of how all that exists is part of the Spirit which gives life to this work. I am humbled and grateful.

To you who have touched my life and been part of the journey: this book would not exist without your loving support. I cannot thank you enough. *Chi-Miigwetch!*

Annie Wenger-Nabigon

November 21, 2021

ABOUT THE AUTHOR

Annie Wenger-Nabigon, Ph.D., is a retired therapist and social work educator. She was born in mountainous southern territory of the Osage Peoples (northcentral Arkansas), the oldest child of Mennonite medical missionaries, and spent most of her childhood years in a Mennonite community in Lancaster, Pennsylvania, the traditional territory of the Susquehannock Peoples. Between the beginning of her story and the current time, she has traveled across many territories, borders and boundaries, always learning, always finding the Light. She is a dual citizen of Canada and the United States, honoring her family on all sides of the borders. She currently resides in Sault Ste, Marie, Ontario.